"This fast-paced, insightful, and readable book provides a wealth of practical advice for how to generate long-term growth through better handling of talent, strategy, and risk."

—**BOB BRADWAY,** Chairman and CEO, Amgen; Board Director, Boeing

"This book is a page-turner based on the experience of three of the best practitioners in their respective fields. It is not 'more of the same' governance and management speak but a great playbook to enhance TSR and sharpen your strategy."

—**GEORGE OLIVER,** Chairman and CEO, Johnson Controls; Board Director, Raytheon Technologies

"What a delight it is to take in the combined wisdom of these three highly respected practitioners of the art of value creation."

—**RON SUGAR,** former Chairman and CEO, Northrop Grumman; Chairman, Uber; and Board Director, Chevron Corporation, Apple, and Amgen

"This book defines the standard for long-term, sustainable value creation with helpful and solid solutions for aligning investors, boards, management teams, and employees. Talent, strategy, and risk will become synonymous with 'total shareholder return.' Well done and a great read!"

—**GREG GARLAND,** Chairman and CEO, Phillips 66; Board Director, Amgen

"A new and thoughtful investor road map for CEOs and CFOs to pay attention to as we navigate issues of talent, strategy, and risk. It's critical that you read this important book."

—**FRANK D'AMELIO,** Chief Financial Officer and Executive Vice President, Global Supply, Pfizer; Board Director, Zoetis and Humana

"Fast-paced and insightful, this book draws on the authors' extensive experience and in-depth interviews with a who's who of business leaders and investors. I intend to regularly return to it as the Power Authority carries out Vision 2030, its new strategic plan."

—**GIL QUINIONES,** President and CEO, New York Power Authority

"A smart and thoughtful narrative filled with keen insights. This book will simultaneously guide you and challenge your thinking about how investors and boards are impacting talent, strategy, and risk in the companies they invest in and oversee."

—**BRUCE BROUSSARD,** President and CEO, Humana; Board Director, KeyCorp

"*Talent, Strategy, Risk* synthesizes and illuminates what really matters to investors. This fast-paced read is a must for CEOs and corporate boards."

—**GREG BROWN,** Chairman and CEO, Motorola Solutions

"The authors provide a rich compendium and a wealth of research around forward-thinking ideas and specific examples of new processes and practices to foster innovation in governance and oversight of today's complex corporations and institutions."

—**IVAN SEIDENBERG,** former Chairman and CEO, Verizon Communications; Board Director, Madison Square Garden Sports; and former Director, BlackRock

"McNabb, Charan, and Carey make a clear, compelling case for boards to rethink the age-old concept of total shareholder return and focus instead on the critical topics of talent, strategy, and risk—hence a newly defined TSR."

—**ROGER FERGUSON,** former President and CEO, TIAA; Board Director, Alphabet, General Mills, and International Flavors & Fragrances

"Attract and empower great talent. Find a leader who can formulate and implement a winning strategy. Foster a culture of intelligent risk-taking. Deliver on these elements of the 'new TSR' and the 'old TSR' will take care of itself. These are the central themes of this powerful book."

—**BRIAN ROGERS,** former Chairman, T. Rowe Price; Board Director, Raytheon Technologies and Lowe's

"The role of the board is more important and demanding than ever. *Talent, Strategy, Risk* helps readers frame and navigate the most important questions with real insights and practical advice—a rare combination these days."

—**KEVIN SHARER,** former Chairman and CEO, Amgen; coauthor, *The CEO Test*

"As a private-company CEO, I found the ideas advanced by the authors to be both refreshingly new and practical. The focus on the emergence of a powerful new ESG investor class was especially relevant."

—**STEPHEN SIDWELL,** CEO, Nexii Building Solutions

"The corporate game is changing from optimizing total shareholder return (TSR) to leading with talent, strategy, and risk, 'the new TSR.' And here, from the A team—Bill McNabb, Ram Charan, and Dennis Carey—is the playbook for directors, executives, and investors to put that future in place now."

—**MICHAEL USEEM,** Professor of Management, The Wharton School; author, *The Edge*

"*Talent, Strategy, Risk* challenges age-old orthodoxies and brings new thinking to how boards manage companies and the investment community."

—**PETER FASOLO,** Executive Vice President, Chief Human Resources Officer, Johnson & Johnson

Talent

Strategy

Risk

*How Investors
and Boards
Are Redefining*
TSR

Talent

Strategy

Risk

Bill
McNabb

Ram
Charan

Dennis
Carey

HARVARD BUSINESS
REVIEW PRESS
BOSTON,
MASSACHUSETTS

Library of Congress Cataloging-in-Publication Data

Names: McNabb, Bill, author. | Charan, Ram, author. | Carey, Dennis C., author.
Title: Talent, strategy, risk : how investors and boards are redefining TSR / Bill McNabb, Ram Charan, Dennis Carey.
Description: Boston, MA : Harvard Business Review Press, [2021] | Includes index.
Identifiers: LCCN 2020057954 (print) | LCCN 2020057955 (ebook) | ISBN 9781633698321 (hardcover) | ISBN 9781633698338 (ebook)
Subjects: LCSH: Boards of directors. | Stockholders. | Corporate governance. | Portfolio management. | Risk management. | Strategic planning—Methodology.
Classification: LCC HD2745 .M365 2021 (print) | LCC HD2745 (ebook) | DDC 658.15/5—dc23
LC record available at https://lccn.loc.gov/2020057954
LC ebook record available at https://lccn.loc.gov/2020057955

ISBN: 978-1-63369-832-1
eISBN: 978-1-63369-833-8

To my Vanguard colleagues: Thank you for all you do on behalf of investors everywhere. You inspire me each and every day.

—BILL McNABB

To the hearts and souls of the joint family of twelve siblings and cousins living under one roof for fifty years, whose personal sacrifices made my formal education possible.

—RAM CHARAN

To the CEOs, boards, and investors who are working on the front lines to build better, high-growth, sustainable, and competitive companies for the benefit of all stakeholders.

—DENNIS CAREY

CONTENTS

Prologue: Changes in the Investment Community
That Led to This Book   *ix*

Introduction: Redefining Corporate Governance
for the Long Term   1

PART ONE

The New TSR

A Framework for Long-Term Management

  1. Talent Rules   17
  2. The Strategic Imperative   45
  3. Managing Risk   69

PART TWO

Best Board Practices

Managing for the New TSR and Long-Term Value Creation

  4. Creating a Capable Board   95
  5. Redesigning the Board's Committees   117
  6. Diversifying Information   133
  7. Engaging with Investors   147

Conclusion: ESG: The Big Picture, Not Just a
Piece of the Puzzle   173

Index   *179*
Acknowledgments   *191*
About the Authors   *195*

PROLOGUE

Changes in the Investment Community That Led to This Book

BY BILL McNABB

Late one evening in the spring of 1986, I sat with a friend on his back porch in Philadelphia. Over a beer and cheesesteaks from Dalessandro's, a city landmark, I began talking about a job offer I had at Vanguard, the mutual fund firm founded by Jack Bogle eleven years earlier.

I told my friend that from the conversations I had with people who worked there—including Bogle and Jack Brennan, the president—it was clear they were building something different. They were passionate about standing up for everyday savers and investors.

Vanguard was unique among investing companies. It was—and still is—the only mutual fund company that is neither publicly owned nor controlled by its founders or a private corporation. Instead it is owned by its clients—the mutual funds it manages, which are in turn owned by the funds' investors. Vanguard's focus is the individual investor, and it is a pioneer of index funds, which buy and hold stocks in perpetuity. But in those days, the firm was still young, and many viewed index investing, while starting to catch on, as a curiosity.

I was twenty-nine, just three years out of Wharton. I'd taught Latin in seventh and eighth grade for two years and coached several sports, then had a brief stint on Wall Street, long enough to understand the model and the mindset there. I knew that Vanguard's structure and its way of thinking was nothing short of revolutionary.

My friend sensed my excitement. "You should take the job," he said. Here was a chance to be part of something I believed in and not let Wall Street tell me what to do.

Some three-and-a-half decades later, Vanguard is still a company that takes a stand for all investors. More broadly, it has been part of a transformation in the way individuals invest, with more and more people around the world investing through index funds and other long-term vehicles.

The Needs of the Long-Term Investor

The nature of investors in the public equity markets has changed significantly over the decades. They are much more focused on the long term today. As of 2020, index funds (including exchange-traded funds) held 41 percent of US mutual fund assets, up from 11 percent in 2000, according to Morningstar.

And index funds have very little turnover. For the Vanguard 500 Index Fund, which tracks the S&P 500 Index, the average annual turnover rate of its portfolio was only 3.6 percent from 2010 through 2019. Meanwhile, US funds that tried to outperform the S&P 500 had an average turnover rate of 65.3 percent over the period, according to Morningstar. Looking at the data another way, the average holding period for a security in the index fund was about twenty-eight years; for the average active fund, it was about eighteen months.

It's important to remember that "the market" is largely composed of real people saving and investing for more secure financial futures. We estimate that individuals own more than three-quarters of the shares in the US stock market, either directly or through mutual funds, based on data from the Federal Reserve and the World Bank.

I often remind people that it's not Vanguard's capital, or Fidelity's capital, or BlackRock's capital. It's the savings and investments of millions of individuals and families, many of whom are investing through 401(k) retirement plans and 529 education savings plans and IRAs. The market is people with long-term goals investing through increasingly long-term investment vehicles.

Now that I've retired from my leadership roles at Vanguard, I've had the chance to serve on the boards of a few public companies. And the experience has given me a better appreciation of the view from both sides of the table. One of my early learnings as a public company director was the importance of understanding the investor base—parsing out the kinds of investors who owned the stock, and why.

Investors can hold shares of a company for a matter of milliseconds, hours, days, months, or even decades. Some investors will make their perspectives known to you; others, you may never know they were there. But no one cares about the long-term health of a company as much as its permanent investors.

At Vanguard, we realized that public companies did not fully appreciate the voice of the long-term investor. The investment infrastructure of the public markets is built on the rhythms of daily stock movements, quarterly reporting cycles, and annual meetings. Index funds don't necessarily participate in that conversation. They are more concerned with long-term governance and board oversight.

At the beginning of this century, firms like Vanguard were known as passive index funds. No one really took governance as seriously as they should—except for early activists. They were beginning to have an undue influence on companies in which they had a far smaller position than ours. And the changes they were pushing were not always in the long-term interest of the company.

That state of affairs led to an awakening at Vanguard and our peers, when we stepped back and said, wait a minute, we are significant long-term holders, if not permanent ones, in some of these companies. And many activists are taking actions that might hurt long-term value for our shareholders. It was time for us to rethink our relationship with the companies in which our shareholders invested through our funds.

Vanguard has always been maniacally focused on its shareholders. If you're an investor there, you're an owner. Index fund managers can't sell the stock of companies they don't like. The only way for an index fund to influence companies is through governance practices. We wanted boards at all companies to be engaged with their owners in the same way we are with ours. That's how Vanguard decided to become more active and more engaged.

One of the crystallizing moments for Vanguard came in 2002, in the wake of the corporate governance failures at Enron, WorldCom, Adelphia, and others. Jack Brennan, by then Vanguard's CEO, wrote to the leaders of 450 companies in which Vanguard funds had substantial equity ownership. His letter laid out Vanguard's expectations on governance matters such as board composition, executive compensation, auditor independence, and shareholder rights.

Those corporate scandals, and the reforms that followed—such as the Sarbanes-Oxley Act of 2002 and the tightening of listing requirements on major stock exchanges—spurred new levels of attention to governance in boardrooms worldwide. But much work was still necessary to build mutual understanding between public companies and their longest-term shareholders.

A number of industry organizations and academic institutions helped to build a bridge. Columbia, Drexel, Harvard, and the University of Delaware regularly hosted forums where large long-term investors, corporate directors, and management teams came together to discuss issues such as the board's role in risk oversight, shareholder engagement, and executive compensation.

I recall a keynote Brennan gave at a Drexel Directors Dialogue event in 2010, in which he told a roomful of corporate directors that they should think of their permanent shareholders as their primary constituency. He said, "At all decision points, the guide star should be: How will this decision affect our permanent shareholders? And does the decision we're making today align our interests with theirs?" At the time, it was a radical message.

In the years that followed, productive dialogues continued between investors and the companies they invested in. Corporate directors gained a deeper appreciation of their longest-term investors. I've told many directors, in gatherings large and small, that index investors like Vanguard are going to hold their stock in good times and in bad. We're not going to second-guess their management decisions quarter by quarter.

But long-term investors do want to know your strategic long-term vision for the company, and how the board's governance aligns with that strategy. Do you have the right directors in place for today and tomorrow? Does the board understand, monitor, and own key risks? Do compensation plans give executives incentives to outperform other companies and create value for long-term investors? Do your shareholders have a voice? And do you listen to it? Those elements can lead to better long-term wealth creation for companies and investors.

The Importance of Capital Markets

When I talk about the importance of governance and good shareholder communication, I do so with full awareness that it's not easy to be a public company. Sometimes I worry that the multitude of requirements placed on public companies has discouraged some startups from going public. Indeed, the number of US public companies has fallen significantly over the past few decades, from more than 8,000 in 1996 to about 4,300 as of mid-2020, according to the World Bank and to analysis by Bernstein Research and Vanguard.

From my perspective, the United States has the most vibrant capital markets in the world. Historically, we've had a good balance between privately held and publicly traded companies. The number of private companies is now on the rise dramatically, in part because falling interest rates over the last twenty years have made borrowing easier, so fewer companies need to go public to raise funds. That's not necessarily a bad thing, but the great aspect of the public markets is that they let everyone benefit from a company's success.

We're concerned that if we're not careful, this balance could be lost. We've observed that some of the best-run public companies operate with a private company mindset. These companies don't focus on hitting a daily stock price or a quarterly earnings target, but on creating business success that they can sustain over generations.

Shareholders and Stakeholders

In the past few years, I've been surprised by the debates about shareholders versus stakeholders. Some have expressed concern that companies are diminishing the importance of shareholder return by paying attention to the needs of other stakeholders. I think this point of view misses the mark entirely.

Being a great employer and a good citizen in your community while staying focused on the client actually leads to better results. At Vanguard, we used to call this the focus on the three Cs—clients, crew, and community. I believe that all companies should think that way, and that doing so is how you create value in the long run. It's not shareholders or stakeholders. It's shareholders *and* stakeholders.

All companies navigate short-run trade-offs that may boost shareholder return. But in the long run, if you want to build great companies, you can't create sustainable shareholder value without providing value to other stakeholders as well.

. . .

The ideas I'm discussing here—maintaining healthy capital markets, leading with a long-term perspective, considering a wide range of stakeholders—are concepts that few people take issue with, like motherhood and apple pie. The trick is putting it all into practice.

With this book, Ram, Dennis, and I try to put these developments into perspective for boards and define the board's new agenda with a set of new practices and guidelines for implementing them.

We don't pretend to have all the answers. That's why, to write this book, we learned from the best. We went out and talked to leading thinkers in public companies, in investing, and in corporate governance. We gathered some of the most innovative and insightful ideas about how to put theory into practice for company directors and executives.

We asked directors how they think about succession planning, board composition, and dealing with a range of stakeholders. We talked to the CEOs of some of the world's largest public companies about how they work with their boards. We talked to leaders of large asset management firms about their expectations of public company boards. We asked activist investors about their views of corporate culture and value creation.

Finally, as we were putting the final touches on this book in late 2020, the world was grappling with the worst pandemic in a century. The wisdom and perspectives that we gathered for this book have taken on an even deeper meaning, especially on matters of risk oversight and the ability to lead organizations with long-term vision, purpose, and resiliency.

We enjoyed learning from this amazing group of leaders. We hope you will, too.

Redefining Corporate Governance for the Long Term

O ver two hundred Business Roundtable CEOs publicly re-buke the idea of shareholder primacy. The world's largest investment management company, BlackRock, requires all companies in its portfolio to demonstrate a path for long-term value creation. Institutional investors, who own 60 percent of *Fortune* 500 companies, expect leaders to keep the short term and long term in proper equilibrium.

Balancing the short term and long term is a perennial struggle, but these new developments—as well as imperatives to emerge stronger from economic crisis, address climate change, and eliminate racial in-equity—put boards squarely at the center and in need of guidance.

To meet these new expectations, what changes do boards need to make? What new principles and practices of corporate governance do we need to lead for the long term? The three of us have been on the front lines of changes in company ownership and in shareholders' ex-pectations of managerial behavior.

As CEO of Vanguard, Bill McNabb helped drive the change in the investment community that owns and evaluates these companies. Bill's efforts date back to 2010, when he first spoke up at a Drexel governance event and left the CEOs in the audience so upset by his suggestion that their boards engage with investors that he thought they were going to throw him out of the room. "They went bananas," he recalls. By 2017, Vanguard had conducted nearly a thousand in-person and virtual meetings on the subject with directors and managers around the world.

In his work as an adviser, Ram Charan has helped boards and senior leaders rethink and redesign their governance practices. Over time, he noted a widening gap between the focus of boards and the concerns of investors, and sharp contrasts between the boards of public companies and those of private and family-owned firms.

As vice chair of Korn Ferry, Dennis Carey has helped reconstitute boards and recruit CEOs to meet the new expectations. He has seen a steady rise in the sometimes-conflicting demands on boards over the years, and he and his Korn Ferry colleagues have conducted extensive research on how boards affect company performance.

We combine our many years of experience working with boards, managements, and the investment community to explain the shifts in perspective and practice that companies must make to escape the traps of short-termism and to drive long-term value creation.

It starts with rethinking total shareholder return and, instead, focusing on a different kind of TSR.

Redefining TSR

For investors, the standard measure of corporate performance is total shareholder return, or TSR—the change in a company's share price with accumulated dividends over time. For boards and for managers, chasing after TSR can put a premium on short-term activities designed to boost the company's stock. The pressure to do so may come from security analysts and the business press, and from activist investors when they think that a company is lagging its market potential.

Yet a focus on TSR brings with it no rules of behavior. Despite their best efforts to build total return, companies continue to make ill-advised mergers, invest in dead-end lines of business, and hire chief executives unsuited to the changing business landscape, all of which hurt shareholders.

Companies got in these straits through shortsightedness, inconsistency, and a focus on the wrong achievements. Companies typically judge each value-creating initiative by its own set of measurements—eyeballs for a content initiative or inventory levels for a manufacturing effort—rather than by a single set of meaningful financial metrics, such as gross margin, revenues, cost reductions, and asset utilization. Timetables are often fuzzy, and accountability for delivering results is typically diffuse, with initiatives placed in the hands of project leaders asked merely to finish the job. CEO pay is often tied to short-term results, not to the success or failure of the seed projects on which the company's future depends. And many boards are oblivious to what management is doing to prepare for the future. All these endemic faults are enemies of long-term value creation.

It's time for companies—led by their boards—to refocus their attention on a new imperative. From the perspective of permanent capital and long-term value creation, we think the best way to create total shareholder return is by focusing on talent, strategy, and risk—the new TSR. (See figure I-1.)

By that we mean first attracting the right talent—the people who you will want to stay, grow, and evolve with you; then creating a strategy that aligns your company not with Wall Street expectations but with the interests of your longest-term investors; and finally, owning at the board level all of the risks that could get in the way of your strategy.

The shift to the new TSR started with investors. As index funds began to assume a more active role in corporate governance, they zeroed in on how management and boards dealt with key corporate

FIGURE I-1

The new TSR

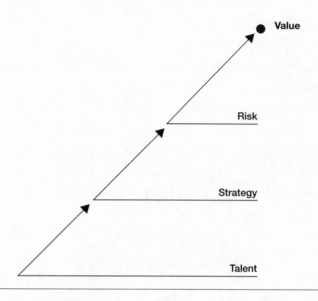

functions, such as selection of the CEO and the leadership team; the steps management is taking to ensure that proposed mergers or changes in strategic direction are worth making; and the measures companies adopt to mitigate and take advantage of risk. In other words, they are looking at talent, strategy, and risk directly, both to protect the company and to enhance its value.

So how did we settle on these three elements as the rightful focus of the board instead of the traditional measure of total shareholder return? Our insight is that an increase in shareholder value is merely an output—the result that managers wish to achieve. We wanted to step back and look at the inputs that generate this output. And the trio of talent, strategy, and risk encapsulate the work of a company, broken down into its discrete functional elements—the functions that the CEO must manage and that the board must oversee to enhance long-term shareholder return. The new TSR is a tool that boards can use to escape from short-termism and reorient for the long term. If the board can get the new TSR right, the old TSR will take care of itself.

Certainly it's what we see work at Vanguard, which is zealously focused on talent, strategy, and risk. Its business may be investing, but it is also a pretty complicated enterprise in its own right, with eighteen thousand employees, offices around the world, and billions of dollars of investment in technology. Vanguard knows firsthand the importance of the new TSR and the ability to execute around it.

The rewards of this new conception of TSR go beyond market gains. Boards can help create a better measure of shareholder value: long-term growth that will benefit both shareholders and society at large. Investors often view social benefits as contrary to financial results—that initiating, say, a zero-carbon strategy will mean higher costs and lower profits. In the short run, that may be true. But such a focus can deliver long-term gains—from future savings and the creation of new lines of business, and from the higher value people will increasingly place on companies that pursue such goals.

Until now, the loudest voices have been skewed toward the near term, and corporate practices have reinforced that perspective. The sanctity of earnings per share, combined with the rhythm of budget and operating reviews, ensures a high degree of myopia. In spite of efforts to balance incentive pay and performance, compensation is still based largely on short-term measures.

In addition, the security analysts who evaluate companies are themselves rewarded for short-term performance. And though shareholder activists are increasingly diverse and have varied time horizons, some are more adept than others at commanding management's attention.

The good news for companies is that institutional investors—the ones who hold some 50 percent to 60 percent of the stock of *Fortune* 500 companies—have found their voice, and they are urging boards to serve as a counterbalance to this short-termism. This book captures their perspectives and presents best practices for boards to streamline their work while meeting the expectations of a broad spectrum of shareholders.

Leading for Tomorrow:
An Example of What We Mean

A board can create tremendous value if it supports decisions that are unpopular in the here and now but are necessary for the company's future. Consider what transpired at PepsiCo in 2013, when the board came under pressure from activist investors to split up the company. Earnings were suppressed and the share price was flat. But CEO Indra Nooyi presented the board with a detailed plan to ensure the company's long-term growth, featuring a shift of resources to emphasize healthier drinks and snacks. After evaluating her plan and monitoring the steps that Nooyi was taking to implement it, including the introduction of new brands, the board decided to back her. The board's confidence in Nooyi and its willingness to stand up to the activists would soon be vindicated: in 2014, PepsiCo began its steady climb to a record share price.

But perhaps the most prominent example of the rewards of a patient board comes from Amazon. CEO Jeff Bezos has always taken a long view, and the board has supported him through initiative after initiative, from expansion of the product line beyond books and unlimited free deliveries for subscribers to video streaming, data management services, and content production. Only a decade ago, critics were complaining that Amazon wasn't generating sufficient profits and wondering when the company would ever make enough money. Now Amazon owns the universe: in the summer of 2020, it became the first company to achieve a trillion-dollar valuation.

With the board's backing, CEOs are more likely to take actions that will pay off in the long term. Without it, they may delay. And worse, any company that wants to invest in its future may be driven into private hands, as Dell Computer was in 2013, when its investor base wouldn't tolerate the effects of a radical shift from the PC business.

Indeed, board inefficacy has become a threat to the existence of public corporations. If a public company fails, it has three choices: a merger with another company, a takeover by private equity, or reformulation to the tune of activist investors. All three have led to a declining number of US public companies. Legal issues and regulation have played a part in the shrinkage, too.

Pressure from activist investors can pose a particular problem for the boardroom. They may threaten to change the CEO or to break up or merge the company with the aim of forcing it to pursue short-term gains instead of building long-term value. If that pattern of privatization takes hold, the capital markets will become a trading venue instead of a capital allocation one, with huge implications for society through the narrowing of the number of people who will be able to participate in creating economic wealth. Boards can be pivotal in arresting this trend.

To preserve their companies, boards can cultivate relationships with the institutional investors who have the largest positions in the corporation. The support of these investors will be crucial to companies as they try to fend off outside forces and achieve their long-term goals. Activists with 2 percent or 3 percent of a company's shares won't be able to have their way without support from some of those institutional investors. This book will teach you how to get them on your side.

Despite the call for boards and CEOs to think more broadly about corporate performance, the competition among companies to create value for their shareholders will remain paramount. But as conditions change, the board must redefine the measure of shareholder value, in collaboration with long-term and permanent shareholders.

In this view, total shareholder return becomes more than just the increase in share price and dividends paid. It also encompasses factors that position the company for long-term growth—such as the quality of a company's market share, its capital efficiency, and its brand. Those are the elements that will determine success in the future.

Besides adopting a longer time horizon, boards must embrace a broader conception of corporate responsibility beyond the immediate financial interests of the shareholders. The Business Roundtable and other voices representing the community at large are asking

corporations to go beyond Milton Friedman's dictum that "the only
. . . social responsibility of business" is "to use its resources . . . to
increase its profits." That, instead, running great companies requires
boards and management to focus on other stakeholders, and doing so
will lead to greater long-term shareholder return.

To successfully steer their companies in new directions, boards must
wrest control from management. Boards have essentially been led by
the CEO's team. They have been almost totally reliant on information
management has provided. As a result, they have been reactive to external change.

Boards must adopt a new modus operandi and mindset. Directors
today function at their best when they are a Zoom meeting away from
one another, not a quarterly meeting away. While they should cultivate
a collegial relationship with management, they must also be independent of it. We will show you how to generate your own sources of
information so that the board can ensure the right balance between
long-term and short-term goals and the interests of all stakeholders.

Talent, Strategy, Risk: The New Board Playbook for Managing for the Long Term

The three of us have watched these trends play out in boardrooms for
years. We based the recommendations in this book on our many years
of experience working on these issues with boards, management, and
the investment community

To write this book, we've talked to dozens of leaders from public and private companies, investment firms, and activist shops. We've
gathered their best insights, and we'll let them share the whys and the
hows of their success. You'll hear from Mary Barra of GM on how to
keep your board engaged, Warren Buffett of Berkshire Hathaway on
how to make a merger, Michele Hooper of the Directors' Council on
CEO succession, Rajiv Gupta of Delphi Automotive on acquisitions,

and more. All are talking about escaping the traps of short-termism and leading for the long term.

The directors, leaders, and investors we interviewed for this book are turning the old way of doing business upside down. The new tools we provide will help you do the same.

In part one, we lay out the framework of the new TSR. We start with talent, in chapter 1. Of all the inputs, talent is the most important. Talent drives strategy and conceives new directions, seizes novel opportunities, and makes corporations more adaptable and agile. Talent manages and mediates risk. It executes plans. Boards can offer crucial support by learning about their company's talent in depth. Then they will be in a position to make recommendations to management about senior leaders and help them face reality about the suitability of staff for short-term and long-term needs, with special emphasis on managing for the long term. You'll hear how the CEO of WSFS Financial Corp. laid the way for his succession by going on the road for three months and putting his heir apparent in charge.

The board's new role in strategy is the focus of chapter 2. In a fast-changing world, setting strategy can no longer be a once-a-year off-site event. It must be an ongoing process, with every meeting an opportunity to challenge the company's strategic framework. We offer a new standard, the moneymaking model, and tie it to long-term goals. You'll read about how GM taps the expertise of board members to help it enter new lines of business. You'll also hear how Delphi Systems focused its portfolio on the businesses that mattered most to its future, how Warren Buffett makes the right decisions about potential mergers, and how boards can help build value for the future by looking out for the interests of all stakeholders.

In chapter 3, we turn our attention to the third leg of the new TSR—risk. Too many companies practice risk avoidance, not risk management. We show how a new focus on risk management shifts the perspective to long-term gains. When properly executed, risk management treats the company as a single system rather than an amalgam of parts. You'll see how Tyco's approach to total enterprise risk helped it survive the financial fraud of its CEO and stave off the threat to its worldwide operations posed by the H1N1 swine flu pandemic of 2009. And you'll read about how Warren Buffett manages audit risk at Berkshire Hathaway.

In part two, we shift to the board's playbook, showing, one by one, the changes in governance that ensue when a board shifts its focus to managing talent, strategy, and risk. (See figure I-2.)

Chapter 4 focuses on the new board capabilities necessary to support long-term value creation. Talent matters not just within the company but also in the boardroom. Most directors have experience in selecting talent along with scars from making wrong decisions, and they have years of collective judgment in taking action. The trick is to learn how to continually adapt to change by having the right mix of talent and fair representation of gender, ethnicity, and age. This chapter will walk you through how to manage these changes. And you'll hear how GM,

FIGURE I-2

The new value playbook

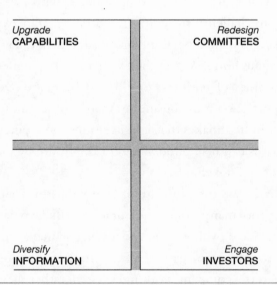

Upgrade
CAPABILITIES

Redesign
COMMITTEES

Diversify
INFORMATION

Engage
INVESTORS

Verizon, and other companies manage the tricky proposition of replacing board members who aren't delivering.

Restructuring board committees is an essential aspect of managing talent, strategy, and risk. In chapter 5, we will show you how division of labor is the only way for directors to use their expertise and achieve the depth of knowledge necessary to do their jobs. For instance, boards have long held that their most important job is selecting the CEO. But if they are going to have a successor ready when they need one, boards must know how to bring talent along. Here you will see why the compensation committee—which we would refashion as the talent, compensation, and execution committee—is best situated to discharge this responsibility. You will read about how Providence Health brought a disrupter from the tech world onto its strategy committee, where he helped transform the company into a health database powerhouse. And you'll see how Wendy's ad hoc technology committee helped turn a burger maker into a digital player, positioned for long-term growth based on a new ordering platform.

In chapter 6, we turn to how boards can diversify the information they have. Reducing the asymmetry of information between the board and management is essential to the board's mission of overseeing talent, strategy, and risk. You'll see how a conscientious CEO like GM's Mary Barra can help keep her board fully informed about the competitive marketplace without pushing her own agenda. You'll learn how GE's board missed out by not digging into the information that could have revealed how badly out of whack its balance sheet was. And you'll see how one exemplary director, Michele Hooper of the Directors' Council, develops her own sources of information by going out on the road by herself.

Finally, to expand on Bill's prologue, in chapter 7 we focus on how boards can engage with investors, a company's most powerful constituency. Here you'll find the culmination of the book's themes as we show you how investors are promoting measures that create value in the long term, with important implications for the board's management of talent, strategy, and risk. You'll see how an activist investor helped DuPont revamp its cost base, capital structure, and portfolio, all to the benefit of long-term shareholder value. And you'll read the terrific tale of Motorola's encounter with the most notorious alpha activist of all.

We've seen how companies that have reinvented their playbooks around these ideas are better prepared to meet the changes in company ownership and in shareholder expectations. We hope this book will help form the basis for a radical new thinking around TSR. Adopting the practices of the new TSR can help you resist short-term pressures and focus on the issues that will let your company thrive, both now and in the future.

PART ONE

The New TSR

A Framework for Long-Term
Management

Talent, strategy, and risk encapsulate the work of a company, broken down into its discrete functional elements—the spheres that the CEO must manage and that the board must oversee, with the aim of enhancing long-term shareholder value. The new TSR is a tool that boards can use to escape short-termism and reorient for the long term. If the board can get the new TSR right, the old TSR will take care of itself.

These three spheres are tightly interrelated. The board must nurture a leadership team suited to create and execute the strategy that the company will need to thrive in the marketplace of the future. And the directors must make sure that the company's strategy both mitigates risks that can threaten the enterprise and embraces risks that present an opportunity for long-term value creation.

The new TSR

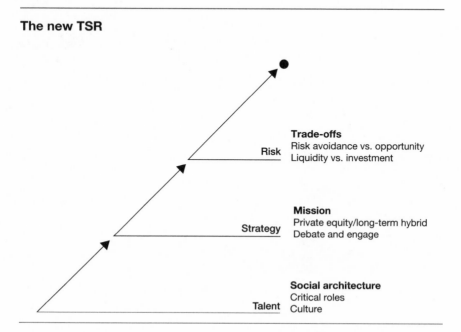

Trade-offs
Risk avoidance vs. opportunity
Liquidity vs. investment

Risk

Mission
Private equity/long-term hybrid
Debate and engage

Strategy

Social architecture
Critical roles
Culture

Talent

Master these three realms—as the first part of this book will show you—and the board will be able to answer the essential question: How does the company grow?

CHAPTER 1

Talent Rules

O f all the factors that go into the creation of long-term value, talent is the most important one for boards to be talking about. More than any financial goal or stratagem, talent—people—determines a company's success or failure. People create and execute strategy and manage the associated risk. They conceive new business opportunities. They allocate resources. They are accountable for sustaining competitive advantage. Indeed, companies don't compete. Talent does.

The priority for talent starts with the CEO, the person of final accountability. So the appointment of the CEO, and oversight of the CEO's tenure, is the board's most important task. That responsibility includes the CEO's top team—the people whose opinions the CEO most respects. This group may number twenty-five or fewer, but their mindset and abilities, and the way in which they invest energy in their work and keep informed, are crucial to the program of the CEO. These people also demand the attention of the board.

Smart companies look for talent everywhere. They vie for talent not only with counterparts in their own business but also with companies in other industries. Established companies compete with startups as well. Around twenty years ago, Amazon CEO Jeff Bezos recruited the chief technology officer of Walmart. That anomalous hire should have been a wake-up call for Walmart, and for Kmart, too. In 2019, Walmart returned the favor and recruited an Amazon staffer to be its chief technical officer. Competitors like Target and Home Depot need to anticipate such moves.

To do so, they have to establish a flow of information about talent. They must follow emerging trends in middle- and upper-level talent, in technology management, in risk and regulatory functions. What trends are new, and what trends are coming? Who is thinking about novel ideas? Such intelligence is second nature in the fashion business, where the move of a designer from one house to another becomes news that spreads instantly throughout the industry. It must become the norm throughout the corporate world.

Yet few boards have this external focus. Exceptional companies like Microsoft recruit regulatory people ahead of time and get them ready to deal with the next wave of oversight. By contrast, the talent development process at old-line players like GE, IBM, Ford, and other *Fortune* 500 corporations has failed. These companies could not produce their own successful candidates despite billions of dollars of development investments. What went wrong?

If talent is to be the board's principal focus, boards need a new approach to its management and oversight. Until recently, most companies had a compensation committee that might meet once a year for half a day, flipping through candidates for top positions, and that would be the end of its scrutiny.

It's time for radical change. Boards at smart companies look at talent every time they meet. At General Motors, CEO Mary Barra opens all board meetings with an executive session that has a human resources management topic on the agenda. She says, "There's always something happening related to talent and people movement or development that I want to keep the board up to speed on." She dedicates one board meeting a year to talent, focusing on CEO succession and development, and discussing in detail the performance of every senior officer of the company.

Others should follow her lead. Companies must lift oversight of talent management to the level of the board, just as they did for audit management. They can start by folding talent development into the ambit of the compensation committee, rechristened as the talent, compensation, and execution committee (see chapter 5). And the board can insist on a greater HR presence in the boardroom, with frequent updates from management and time to make its own observations.

In this chapter, we will present the lessons of leaders who have made talent their priority. (See figure 1-1.)

FIGURE 1-1

The new TSR: Talent

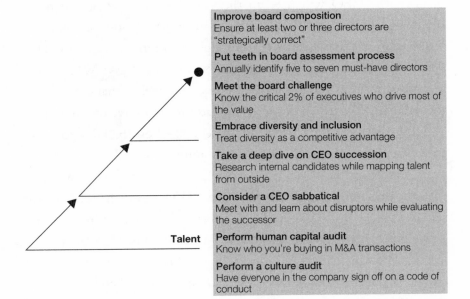

Improve board composition
Ensure at least two or three directors are "strategically correct"

Put teeth in board assessment process
Annually identify five to seven must-have directors

Meet the board challenge
Know the critical 2% of executives who drive most of the value

Embrace diversity and inclusion
Treat diversity as a competitive advantage

Take a deep dive on CEO succession
Research internal candidates while mapping talent from outside

Consider a CEO sabbatical
Meet with and learn about disruptors while evaluating the successor

Perform human capital audit
Know who you're buying in M&A transactions

Perform a culture audit
Have everyone in the company sign off on a code of conduct

Talent

A CEO for the Long Term

No job of the board is more important to the creation of long-term value than selecting the CEO and the leadership team. Their capabilities must align with both where the company is today and where it is headed. The CEO does more than run the business. The CEO is your long-term visionary. As former WSFS Financial Corp. chair and CEO Mark Turner says, "The CEO is developing into not just a leader of the organization but a leader of leaders—an external champion and explorer for the organization and a serial disrupter."

But first, boards must disrupt the old way of choosing the CEO. Gone are the days when the board could simply nod through the incumbent's pick for the job, perpetuating yesterday's rule. In choosing the CEO, whether from inside or outside the company, the board must focus relentlessly on the long-term needs of the company.

To meet these needs, the board can start by deepening its understanding of the company's talent pool. It should also determine the qualities the CEO will need in the years ahead based on emerging trends in the marketplace. And the board must take into account the vagaries of succession, ranging from a planned retirement to a sudden departure. Among the questions the board should ask: What is the second-generation pool? What is the generation below that group? Will the company have three or four candidates ready in five or ten years?

The board must know these candidates and follow their development path. If every year the CEO says she's going to stay for the next five years, the board must search for candidates deeper in the corporation than the person in the office next to the CEO because the CEO might outlast the person next door. That's why smart companies make talent development part of their agenda. For instance, J.P. Morgan Asset & Wealth Management takes the top team away for a week every summer and dedicates an entire day to talent. All boards should consider asking their CEO to do the same.

This sort of strategic thinking is key to managing for the long term. Throughout the process of evaluation, boards should look forward, not backward, which means letting go of assumptions about the candidates they are trying to assess. A lot of boards fall into the trap of confusing familiarity with actual assessment of a candidate. It's ironic that at a time of so much transformation in business, boards don't challenge themselves to look at transformational CEO candidates wherever they happen to come from. Elena Botelho, senior partner at leadership advisory firm ghSMART, says, "When you see a board making the wrong decision, it's typically because they thought they were making a 'safe choice.'"

Familiarity is not data. To move in the right direction, start by jettisoning the old system of internal assessments. From where we sit, the board has too often simply taken the recommendation of the outgoing CEO without getting data on up-and-comers. Enlisting the help of an outside consultant can give you more perspective on future needs.

The boards that succeed at CEO succession link their requirements to strategies. They step back and take a fact-based, analytical view on a broad range of candidates. Often the best candidate for succession turns out to be an outlier instead of the obvious choice. Data-driven analysis of company needs will encourage greater objectivity and let boards come to a reckoning with their unspoken assumptions before an outsider forces the issue.

Some companies are using simulations to test how a candidate would act when presented with scenarios that a CEO might face on the job. Simulations also let companies benchmark candidates against one another. Humana, for instance, used simulations before appointing Bruce Broussard CEO in 2013. Doing so gave the outgoing CEO and the board a window on how the various candidates would respond to different challenges, based on hard data beyond interviews alone.

To make a choice for the long term, consult the team below the CEO, which often knows a lot more about the candidate pool than the CEO does. Inevitably, the CEO wants their lieutenant to be the successor. The board has a fiduciary responsibility to understand who out there might be a better pick.

At GSK, when Jean-Pierre Garnier was retiring as CEO in 2008, three insiders were in the running for the job, and the board formed a clear bias to anoint the person who was sitting in the office just next door to him. So one of us (Carey) identified fourteen executives within the company who had interacted with all three candidates, flew around the world to interview them, and asked which of the three they thought would be the best choice for the future. And nearly 100 percent of them recommended the same person—Andrew Witty, one of the other two insiders. Witty got the job.

This model is one that every company can adopt to vet an internal CEO candidate. At GSK, the data from the review changed the decision of the board that had already made up its mind to accept the recommendation of the CEO. Listen to the people who have worked with your internal candidates. Conduct a systematic, thorough canvassing of close colleagues and customers who have worked with them. In so doing, you will turn a rote anointment of a CEO's recommendation into a hard-nosed selection process.

If you are nearing a decision on an internal successor, give the candidates a chance to show how they might manage the agenda of the future. Then you can base your decision on real-world information, like quality of decision making in a fast-changing world. One approach is to put your candidates through their paces in different parts of the company. Then you can see how they operate in challenging circumstances and cope when confronted with competitive issues. And the board can become confident that the next CEO will know how to build an effective team, make good and timely decisions, and lead the company in the right direction.

Just before Mark Turner of WSFS stepped down as CEO, he spent three months on the road looking for opportunities to ally with innovative companies. He took advantage of his time away to field-test his heir apparent. (For more on his sojourn, see chapter 2.) For the previous three years, he had moved his number two, Rodger Levenson, through various roles, from chief commercial lender to chief financial officer to head of corporate development working on mergers and acquisitions. The natural progression would be for Levenson to become chief operating officer, with responsibility for Turner's direct reports. Turner put that plan in motion just before he left.

Turner says, "While I was gone, he ran the organization. He stepped into my role. He did the earnings calls, did the weekly staff meetings, did the monthly strategy meetings, ran two board meetings as the effective CEO, and did everything that was necessary to keep the organization moving forward." The period was an active one for the company, involving the negotiation and closing of three small acquisitions. So his role was more than stewardship. Turner adds, "It became a way for me, for the board, and for him to decide if this is something he can do and something he wanted to do."

The tryout also demonstrated the strength and cohesiveness of WSFS's team. Turner says, "While it was a contained test of leadership, it was also a test of the model we'd been using for a while, which is dispersed leadership. Rodger and his team stepped up and did incredibly well because they were used to being leaders. This was not an abrupt change in authorities or responsibilities."

What is more, Turner's absence from the office helped other leaders develop. He says, "We had a couple of very new members of the team, one a very young CFO, and he blossomed during that time because he was lifted and asked to do more than he otherwise would have. Had I been there, he would have been two steps from the top. Now he was only one step away and was asked to do much, much more."

Field-testing CEO candidates has become a hallmark of long-term planning. Any venture that lets board members see candidates in a live environment is invaluable. How do the potential leaders deal with stress? How do they perform with the full weight of responsibility on their shoulders? Only then will you be able to see if they can act calmly and thoughtfully when the shells are exploding around them.

CEO Succession Is a Judgment Call

For the wreckage that can ensue when the board gets succession wrong, look no further than Ford's performance over the past twenty years. After a period of good returns and market share, in 2001 the board asked CEO Jacques Nasser to resign after he clashed with chairman William Ford over strategy and corporate values. Ford, the great-grandson of the founder, had become chair two years before, and with the family trust holding 40 percent of the vote, the CEO role was his for the taking. He took it.

What followed was a period when the board's passive approach to CEO succession resulted in a string of failures. Ford, not a natural chief executive, relied heavily on his COOs. He, and the board, cycled through three in five years, a huge turnover rate for the executive wing. Collectively they racked up $22 billion in debt. Ford finally told the board to hire a new CEO.

It delegated the job to two board members with a good track record in selecting CEOs—Irv Hockaday, CEO of Hallmark Cards, and John Thornton, co-president of Goldman Sachs. In 2006, they recruited Alan Mulally from Boeing, where he had overseen the creation of the 777, the top-selling wide-body jet, and demonstrated his ability to execute strategy and lead large teams. One of us (Carey) conducted Mulally's vetting.

There was no purge when Mulally arrived. He succeeded because he was a good leader. On his first day, in a meeting with two dozen executives, someone asked him why he should be CEO of Ford. He said, "You're a great team, and you've taken this company to disaster. I'm going to work with you to take this company to new heights." Over his eight-year tenure, he paid off most of Ford's debt; sharpened the company's focus by unloading Jaguar, Volvo, and Land Rover; built up market share; and restored the stock price. He stepped down in 2014.

In the years since, however, the board repeated the mistakes that had sent the company to its nadir. Hockaday and Thornton were gone from the board by the time Mulally stepped down. The board appointed his choice for successor: Mark Fields, the COO. He was an able executive, and Ford's profits were good on his watch, but sales declined 25 percent, a steeper fall than the industry average, and share price fell by 35 percent. The board asked him to leave after only three years.

Next came Jim Hackett, a former CEO of Steelcase, the furniture maker. His experience might make him seem a strange choice to lead an automaker. Ford's chair—still company scion Bill Ford—didn't think so, and he gave Hackett the job without much input from anyone else or a systematic search. Three years later, after billions in losses and a 40 percent decline in share price, Hackett was fired.

Ford's board chose a new CEO in late 2020, its third in six years, and still doesn't have a settled strategy. The board, and the chair, failed in their most important job: selecting, developing, and retaining a CEO. Collectively the board destroyed shareholder value and, through plant closures, the lives of employees, suppliers, and whole communities.

What a difference the board can make when it gets things right. A prime example of an expertly conceived and executed succession plan culminated in Coca-Cola's 2016 appointment of James Quincey. Few were surprised by the choice of this high-performing company veteran. But what outsiders didn't know was how deeply the board was involved in developing him and the next generation of leaders.

Two decades before, Coke had been caught short when longtime CEO Roberto Goizueta suddenly died. The ones who came after him were not terribly successful, exposing gaps in a leadership team that the board had assumed was strong. Even worse, the board had been disconnected from the succession process, ceding the job to the incumbent. As former senator and long-serving Coke board member Sam Nunn observed, "When things are going well, it's easy to become a little complacent. You assume you will continue to have strong leadership, until you find out too late that there are gaps."

To help ensure that potential leaders would get the opportunities they needed to grow, in the early 2000s the board created a management development committee to oversee talent for senior positions and

CEO succession, with investor Herb Allen as its chair. The primary focus of the committee was on the twenty top positions, but the committee looked several levels down in the company, too.

The committee members told the incumbent CEO, Muhtar Kent, that they wanted to get to know key people around the world. Kent arranged for one leader to attend each committee meeting, where the visiting leaders discussed the business and answered questions about their part of the world. Nunn says, "I always wanted to know what the person thought about political changes in the region and chances for conflict. I was trying to gauge their grasp of things beyond how many bottles of Coca-Cola were sold."

The committee also ventured into the field to see leaders—and potential CEO candidates—in action, sometimes spending a whole day on these visits. While visits to headquarters revealed how leaders related upward, the site visits showed how they related to their team. As Nunn explains, "A leader who interrupts or edits everything means one of two things. Either they don't have confidence in their people or their ego is too big for their position."

Throughout this process, the board was able to get a close look at a handful of potential successors years before Kent's scheduled retirement. Especially important was the interaction between the development committee, the full board, and the CEO. No party pushed a favorite onto the others. Allen says, "As we continued to meet with the candidates, Muhtar never said or implied, 'This is the person who is about to be my successor.'" Rather all parties pooled their judgment to identify leaders and assess their potential.

When the board met candidates who it liked, Kent became their champion. Kent saw the company as a living organism, which means the leader must be able to change it. "That requires testing leaders in new roles to see how they adapt," he says. "So we created those assignments, and quickly made a change if it didn't work out." For example, Kent elevated two people to new roles with a much greater degree of complexity. Within two years, he concluded that neither would be right for the top job.

By then, Kent's retirement was two years away and the list of potential successors was shorter, so the board focused on the essential criteria for the job. One of the central characteristics of the beverage business is the centrality of the bottlers, each of which is a multibillion-dollar business in its own right. So a key requirement of the CEO—and one reason the board preferred internal candidates—is having the right background, credibility, and intellectual heft to influence the bottlers, for if the bottlers don't invest, Coke's business cannot grow.

That criterion would prove crucial to Quincey's ascension. Kent first met his eventual successor in 2005, when Quincey was in Argentina as president of Coke's South Latin American division. With the development committee's blessing, Kent moved him to Mexico. "That's when I really started noticing," says Kent. "Every time I visited the country, I saw that the bottlers were happy, customers were happy, and results were good." By 2013, Quincey was running the company's European operations.

Coke also needed someone who could react quickly to shifting circumstances, such as changing views about diet and health. Here Nunn's firsthand observations of Quincey proved invaluable. He recalls, "When James did a tour of one of the bottling plants and we were talking to people, I saw in him a willingness to confront reality." Especially with a brand that has been so successful for such a long time, the ability to see that the company now needed new products to thrive would be essential.

With the development committee and the board in agreement, Kent made Quincey president and chief operating officer—his final test. There he proved that he could make smart decisions about new products, think strategically, identify talent, and act like a leader. In December 2016, the board announced that he would be the next CEO.

Allen observes, "I have been through five CEO successions. This is the best selection process I've seen. We had all the data we needed and were able to bring the best judgment to bear." The process was natural and rigorous and, above all, patient and well thought out. Most of all, the plan worked because the board devoted years to getting it right.

Keeping the CEO on Track

In its role of overseeing CEO performance, the board must be predictive, watching for signs of faltering leadership, especially short-termism. CEOs are good at looking forward and back six months. That is not long-term thinking. How to check this from the boardroom? Look for anomalies in the operating statements. Did management shift marketing expenses from one quarter to the next to help meet its numbers for analysts? Or book sales from the next quarter to this one? Or forgo investment necessary to build for the future? Or fail to face up to the need to remove a high-level person, or contemplate a questionable acquisition? These are all red flags.

Those are the moments for the board to sense what is happening, step in, and advise—say, by encouraging the CEO to tell the truth if execution has failed or if the company has borrowed from next year. Roger Ferguson, CEO of insurance services provider TIAA, says, "The board is rethinking its function to serve more as coach, with more engagement below CEO, more informal communications between meetings, and more data."

Smart boards are remaking the way in which they deliver performance assessments. A common practice has been to evaluate the CEO via a set of questions, perhaps twenty or so, on which the directors rate the CEO on a scale of one to five. The chair of the governance committee would then meet with the CEO to deliver the compiled results, along with written comments. It's a process that is often offensive to the CEO, and quite ineffective.

A better approach is to generate a list of suggestions from the independent directors for how the CEO can improve performance. The chair and head of the compensation committee would then discuss these ideas with the CEO. The suggestions must be insightful and constructive. For instance, "Your CFO is a good person, but maybe you ought to rethink the role." The message is not that the CEO must fire the CFO but that the CFO is not performing well; perhaps the CEO has a blind spot here. The CEO would then be primed for a fruitful discussion with the CFO.

Other observations from the directors might involve judgment about a project, external trends or relationships, a lack of investment, concerns about human resources, customer issues, or inattention to a new regulation. Such feedback can be a gift to the CEO. It is the sort of advice a CEO wants—congenial and collegial, independent but like a partnership.

Don't base decisions about the CEO's future on factors unrelated to performance. For example, boards are also social organizations, which can complicate efforts to replace the CEO. As a result, often an amiable but mediocre performer is allowed to stay in the post. If the CEO and the board members are friends, and the CEO has treated the directors well, making a change will be very difficult for the board and require a lot of fortitude.

Difficult or not, if your CEO is under fire, the best course is to be honest about it in public. Don't say that you have total confidence in the CEO, only to fire that person three months later. Your board, and your company, will lose credibility. Such was the case at beleaguered aircraft manufacturer Boeing, where chair David Calhoun became CEO within weeks of expressing support for then-incumbent Dennis Muilenberg.

The board mustn't shrink from the hard choice or make a new appointment out of fear. Michele Hooper, CEO of the Directors' Council and board member at PPG and UnitedHealth Group, says, "There's always a leap of faith when you select somebody to sit in the CEO chair. But you have done enough homework, and you keep your fingers crossed that over time your decision proves correct."

Creating the Leadership Team

The development of talent throughout the organization is a much bigger part of the CEO's responsibility than it was twenty or thirty years ago. The board can help by ensuring that the company is organized to support the CEO in this role. If the head of human capital isn't a direct report to the CEO and one of the top two or three highest-paid people in the company, you probably aren't putting enough emphasis on talent development.

The best CEOs think of their senior team members as partners. One of us (McNabb) used to welcome new members of the leadership team by saying, "Congratulations. Your day job is partnering with me to run Vanguard. Your night job is leading HR," or whatever unit the person had been hired to manage.

For that reason, talent at levels below the C-suite should be a major focus of the board. As we describe in our book *Talent Wins* (by Ram Charan, Dennis Carey, and Dominic Barton), the most important task is to identify and cultivate the critical 2 percent—or the critical two hundred, in larger corporations—those crucial leaders responsible for managing the great preponderance of a firm's value-creating activities. The work and vision of these people will determine your strategy, direction, and success. Successful organizations thrive by relying on this key talent.

As with the CEO, boards must be forward-looking in evaluating talent throughout the company. Ed Garden, founding partner of investment firm Trian Partners, points out that the compensation committee deals mainly with the top twenty executives in the corporation, but the companies Trian invests in might have 50,000, or 100,000, or 300,000 employees. He asks, "How do you ensure across the organization that you're attracting the best people, identifying the real talent, and moving them up and giving them blue sky? And who is developing them? And how do you do that at the board level? What core competence must go? What new core competence is needed? What is the transition?"

One failing of many development programs is that they are designed to teach about and celebrate past and present successes instead of preparing executives to meet new competitive challenges. Management and the board then end up assessing who they need based on where the company is now and not where it should be in the future. If the requirements of the corporation are changing, boards must identify the skills and experiences they will need tomorrow. And they have to ask whether the current leaders can make the transition to a new way of thinking and operating.

Smart companies are employing new techniques to make just this sort of determination. Some startups have used short, interactive simulations to assess candidate performance and behavior. Companies hiring technical talent increasingly rely on public competitions to identify high performers who traditional recruitment methods would miss— say, those living in another country. And larger players, including Google, McKinsey, and Korn Ferry, are investing in performance analytics to develop predictive talent algorithms like the ones that sports teams have used with great success to identify players likely to be high performers in their position.

Other companies are jettisoning old ways of performance evaluations. For instance, the current popular system of 360-degree assessments—which entails feedback from subordinates, colleagues, and supervisors plus a self-evaluation—is internally focused and not very good at predicting how an executive will perform in the next role up. We recommend a 450-degree assessment, with the final 90 degrees conducted by a neutral party that gathers data confidentially about executives to predict how they would likely perform in advancing the company's strategy in the years ahead and meeting its major challenges and goals.

Given the fast-changing nature of business in a time of emergency, skill development is apt to be the biggest part of the talent budget. Companies should gear some training initiatives to the moment and focus others on the future. Each should get a separate line of the budget. The CFO and the chief of HR should collaborate on the appropriate amount to allocate.

If need be, the board should challenge the leadership budget. GE did not provide a development path for its leaders, sacrificing long-term growth opportunities. Demand a framework for training and development—not just the budget number, but how the budget is spent, and what is the projected return.

Just as strategy is, the attributes of leadership can be company-specific. Turner of WSFS says, "Certain qualities of a leader cut across all organizations. But depending on the culture and style of the organization, to be a good leader at WSFS might look tremendously different from being a good leader at Citibank." So his company developed a program about how to be a successful leader at WSFS. Managers learn not only general leadership skills but also how the company differs from its peers.

To prepare for tomorrow, good boards keep abreast of talent trends in their industry. For instance, the auto industry is shifting its priorities from mechanical engineering talent to software and electrical engineering talent. As a result, GM's board spent a session with the head of product development and talked about how to hire talent that fit the changing nature of the business. The key to such sessions? Turn them into discussions, not presentations. CEO Mary Barra will prep the board ahead of time by sending them information about industry trends. And she makes sure that top people in the organization have a chance to interact with the board.

The changing of the guard in the employee base is also affecting the talent proposition. Board members should consider not only the strategic disruption arising from technology but also the upheaval in demographics as companies deal with a multigenerational employee base. As baby boomers begin to retire, companies need to bring in new talent with different skills and mindsets. So besides overseeing long-term strategy, boards must also focus on how to build the talent pool to execute it.

Such changes have driven the talent discussion to the forefront for board members. It's no longer enough for the board to talk once a year about the management development program. The directors need to discuss where they want the company to be five years from now. What does that strategy look like? What talent base will you need? In many cases, the need is for different skills, different energy, and a different culture.

The board should insist that management assess its talent development program and communicate its findings to the board—identifying the people who advance to positions where they made a difference. Former Vanguard CEO Jack Brennan experienced that oversight first-hand. When he was running the company, his technology chief died suddenly, and he told the board that he was going to go outside the company for a new head. A director suggested that he consider the person who ran Vanguard's internet unit. Brennan demurred because the candidate was only thirty-one. The director said, "When you were thirty-one years old, you were running the whole company."

Today Brennan says, "I didn't have the brains or the courage to put a thirty-one-year-old in charge of a third of the company." The board can help managers make difficult decisions on talent when they can't quite pull the trigger. An epilogue to this story: that young IT leader was Tim Buckley, who would succeed Bill McNabb as Vanguard CEO almost two decades later.

One technique we like for bringing talent along is rotating key managers through different roles, which will broaden their experience, improve their learning skills, and help them apply their expertise in new circumstances. Properly managed, these talent pools will be the source of new team leaders. But each rotation must involve more than a couple of years of ticket punching. They have to last long enough— three or four years—so that the staff member can demonstrate real accomplishment and a broadening of their ability to manage on a larger scale, at a higher degree of complexity, or with a greater level of responsibility.

Some companies offer the prospect of job rotation as a hiring tool and use their young employees to sell the idea. For recruitment drives at colleges, GM will often use staffers who have graduated within the past five years. Newcomers can participate in a two- or three-year program that will move them through different areas of the company.

The automaker has learned that young staffers appreciate the chance to experience a variety of roles as they enter a company as big as GM.

Board members will need to keep track of promising newcomers as they develop. To get to know the talent in an organization, venture beyond the sort of meet-and-greet events orchestrated by management. For example, companies often have analyst days, when they roll out the next generation of leaders or key executives in the management structure. And while such sessions are sometimes helpful, they can involve a lot of artifice. Most of these presentations are very polished and well scripted, and don't give you a real view of what's going on in an organization.

Instead, board members should spend time with key employees on their own and in informal settings. Bob Weismann, former director of Pitney Bowes, instituted a policy whereby directors would have breakfast with two employees before every board meeting. He finds the arrangement better than a formal dinner with board members and management sitting at a long table, which is good for presentations but leads to scattershot conversations. (For that reason, former Verizon CEO Ivan Seidenberg always insisted on round tables.)

Field visits are especially useful in letting board members see several layers down and get to know the people most likely to be the leaders of the future. Many boards use employee engagement surveys to probe what the lower levels of the company feel about how leaders are managing their responsibilities. Smart directors will leave the office instead and get out into the organization without management looking over their shoulders. Then they can get a better sense of what's actually going on.

Use such opportunities not only to ask questions but also to let employees ask questions of you. UnitedHealth Group board member Michele Hooper has followed this model when running town halls for employees on her own. "They will come out and ask you the darnedest things," she says. "I've been put on the spot about individuals or company strategy. Always leave enough time at the end to say, 'Is there anything else you want to ask me, or tell me, or talk about?' That always elicits something that's not on the agenda but gives me an insight into what they're thinking and how they're feeling about their organization and their leadership."

Informal settings can also help board members get a better reading from the CEO about talent. The aim should be to encourage a free flow of ideas about how to create a leadership team from scratch. Such a meeting wouldn't involve any shuffling of documents—it would just be conversation, and preferably over dinner instead of in the boardroom, because the moment the talk becomes formal, the CEO will start to protect the team.

To assess talent at Tyco International, former CEO Ed Breen, now executive chair of DuPont, would arrange a dinner with division heads and ask them to bring along some staffers responsible for the day-to-day work. He would then assign three or four directors to visit a site on their own for a whole day with the unit's management team and local employees. The night before, board members would have dinner with 150 people from the local site, letting directors see how much the workforce was engaged with the objectives of the company.

Intelligence from outsiders can also give you insight into your management team and a sense of how they will perform in the future. Talk to investors at your customer events. You'll get a better sense of what the outside world thinks of your talent, and who will excel in different circumstances. The people who perform well when the company is in a steady state may not be the ones best suited for leading in a transformational era.

Whether the top talent is homegrown or imported, smart boards stay ahead of trouble on their leadership team, keeping them on track for the long term. Use board meetings to assess performance of important players below the level of the CEO and be ready to step in and offer coaching. In one successful intervention, the board of a $9 billion industrial company in the southwestern United States followed a standard board meeting with an hour-long executive session. In the session, it discussed the contributions of some of the key managers. Among the observations:

—The head of manufacturing is spread too thin and not up to par. He is focused on operations and cannot plan five years out.

—The head of a major business unit is not seeing the potential for exponential growth. We need someone with a broader view of what could be a $10 billion business.

—The people identifying acquisitions missed the services area.

As a result, presentations to the board in the next six months became clearer, crisper, and more to the point, showing greater cooperation among the team.

Retaining the Right Talent: Compensation, Diversity, and Sustainability

As part of its oversight, the board must ensure that the compensation system is fairly conceived and implemented, and that it is calibrated to retain essential staff.

In managing the CEO's compensation, it's the responsibility of the board to ensure that CEO pay is not out of line. The greater the complexity of the package, the harder it is to strike the right balance. Warren Buffett says,

> I was on the board of one very prominent company where the CEO's options were excessive. They were fifteen years and tilted every possible way. And the directors never specifically approved them. The CEO never lived big, but he thought he was the best CEO in the country, and he felt that if he wasn't paid accordingly, he just wasn't being given proper recognition—a very human failing. I think that picking the right CEO is ten times more important than the compensation. But somebody has to be

there to represent the shareholders in terms of overreaching by even very competent executives.

Consultants can help you set compensation levels based on the competitive landscape, but they can only take you so far. You need directors who are business-savvy and owner-oriented, with a particular interest in the corporation. Only then will somebody on the comp committee speak up when CEO pay is out of line.

Forward-thinking companies will link compensation to initiatives that build the future. It is the board's role to insist that management always considers the long term in recruitment and retention. If an executive is crucial to the future development of a key line of business, the board must ask management if it is paying her well enough because she is someone the company will want to stay for ten years. Are you, the management, doing enough for her?

Larger corporations may need to vary compensation level by sector. In 2015, when GM acquired Cruise, a developer of self-driving cars, the unit had forty employees. It now has about eleven hundred. The company has a different compensation structure for that division. Given its work and its research, Cruise competes not as much with Toyota and Volkswagen as with Google, Facebook, and Amazon. And that's right out of Silicon Valley. Investments in the unit by SoftBank and Honda let GM directly compensate employees by issuing stock, which gave the company a way to put a value on Cruise's growth.

Be ready to adapt your compensation structure to take account of new preferences. GM has found that for millennials, benefits are equally important as pay, along with where and how they work. So the company regularly benchmarks its compensation programs and assesses whether they are attuned to the newest cohort of employees.

Make sure your talent does not grow stale and remains engaged. Turner of WSFS recommends that all companies send executives on an extended tour every three to five years as part of talent refreshment, as he did himself shortly before he retired (see chapter 2). He advises starting with the CEO and then switching to other senior managers to give each a chance to recharge their batteries. We all approach the world from different perspectives, so the CEO's insights from the tour will differ from the head of human capital's and the chief technology officer's.

Most board members know that companies should do more to ensure diversity in their talent pool. One executive asked the management of a large corporation to analyze staff by gender and race deep down in the organization. The results were disappointing, and to the detriment of the company as well as the employee base. The executive asks, "If 1.5 percent of your VPs are Black, are you finding the best people?"

For that reason and more, companies must recalibrate their whole policy of recruitment around diversity. At Vanguard, one of us (Mc-Nabb) was looking to hire a general counsel because our longtime incumbent retired. We felt that we needed to go outside to find someone with even greater breadth, especially in light of the evolving globalization of our business. We went to Spencer Stuart, the search firm, which proposed some solid candidates, but essentially all of them were white men. The investment management business is not a very diverse one.

We finally went back and said, "We won't make a hire until you show us legitimate candidates of diversity. And unless you do, we will keep the position open." Spencer Stuart eventually brought us some good candidates, including one incredible woman who happened to be Black. We were able to lure her to Philadelphia from New York. It took us four months longer than we'd planned, but she has made us so much better than we would have been if we hadn't taken those steps. Make no mistake: She wasn't hired because she was Black. In my mind, she blew away all the candidates with her experience and potential. The lesson is that we would never have found her had we not insisted on a diverse pool.

Talent exists in every sector of society. We don't have to prove diversity as a value creator. Diversity has to be at the center of recruitment. To create diversity, companies must transform a fundamental premise of recruitment: rather than simply seeking the best candidate when a position opens, the people in charge of hiring must change the selection process to identify talented people early in their careers. Instead of the usual process of waiting to find a general counsel until the position opens, companies must shift to one where they dig through layers to find raw talent long before they have to make an appointment.

Boards must change their mindset to make sure the company stays ahead of such needs instead of reacting to whatever the CEO serves on their plate. View talent through a wide-angle lens. Boards need to ensure not just diversity of gender, ethnicity, and age—all legal imperatives—but also diversity of thought, geography, and experience. Use nontraditional talent pools. Beware of unconscious bias, or bias built into algorithms.

Diversity should be real, not simulated—that is, the hiring of people to let you tick off boxes. Mary Erdoes of J.P. Morgan says, "Diversity for diversity's sake doesn't get you anywhere. Diversity of thought, which comes from diversity of age, experience, industry—that's the most valuable, hands down." Those are the outsider perspectives that let people ask the so-called dumb question, "which is never dumb," says Erdoes.

Increasingly, companies are recognizing that women already on their staff are in undervalued positions and could be playing a wider role across the corporation. Senior women in many US companies are concentrated in HR departments, often at the highest level. In 2019, the chief human resources officer (CHRO) at fifty-eight of the *Fortune* 100 companies was a woman. Increasingly the CHRO is deeply involved in planning the company's future. Yet the HR function is generally still thought of as a softer role than other senior positions and less transferrable to elsewhere in the C-suite.

Smart companies are helping senior women expand their ambit by forming a G3, or group of three—a partnership of the CEO, the CFO, and the CHRO. They jointly set priorities and review the company's operations every quarter and communicate frequently in between. The tight working relationship links the allocation of human and financial resources across the organization and vastly improves strategy and execution.

The same idea can apply at lower levels in the organization. HR leaders can cultivate broader skills by working closely with leaders of business units, helping improve placement, recruiting, and learning and development of senior women. All these initiatives can also help to identify HR leaders who have the potential to serve on public boards (see chapter 4).

At GM, every board meeting has a diversity element, featuring a deep dive into one aspect of the issue—focusing on women at one meeting, on nonwhite talent at another, on talent outside the United States at the next. Whenever managers travel to a plant in another country and board members are along for the trip, the agenda will always allow time for the directors to meet with local leaders so they can see up-and-coming talent.

The emerging goals of sustainability and social responsibility are important for talent as well. While some companies promote sustainability as part of philanthropy, others, like Unilever, have said that sustainability will define who they are. Many companies lie in between. But, says Shelly Lazarus, chair emeritus and former CEO of Ogilvy & Mather, the shift is toward the Unilever side of the house: "The more millennial your communities and your audiences and your workforce are, the more it matters." To millennials, this issue is truly important, and you ignore it at your peril. They have strong opinions about which companies are good and which ones are bad. And they use these judgments when deciding whether to join a company or to stay where they are.

Unilever has reaped the rewards of its policy. Its sustainable living plan has been great for attracting millennials to work there. Talent is scarce, and millennials favor Unilever as the second-best place in the world to work, after Patagonia.

Yet not all see the bottom line as the be-all and end-all of sustainability measures. Former Xerox CEO and current Johnson & Johnson board member Anne Mulcahy says, "Sustainability and social responsibility are not inconsistent with shareholder value, but I don't think we should discuss corporate citizenship in the context of financial returns. It's hugely important to the employee value proposition, but it's largely becoming a broader employee expectation, which I think is really quite positive." (For more on sustainability, see chapter 2.)

Tracking Culture

Culture is an essential part of the talent equation. Culture is the ethos of your business. It informs behavior. It shapes talent. But culture is not static. It is also informed by the people you bring into the fold.

The implications of cultural problems resound throughout the corporation. Many of the big corporate failures of recent years—Wells Fargo, Enron, Volkswagen, and Boeing, and the #MeToo issues that have affected many organizations—are not simply failures of risk oversight but are borne of cultures where values are misaligned, the wrong things are rewarded, or people are fearful or reluctant to report wrongdoing. Tim Richmond, CHRO of biopharmaceutical company AbbVie, says, "Culture is at the heart of everything, whether it's people's choices to take property or damage the company's reputation or not care about it. Culture is not a program. It's a reflection of what you do every day. How you engage. How you react."

To make sure the culture is healthy, board members of every company should conduct a culture audit, and to do it well, directors must get out in the field. They will learn a lot more about culture on a site visit than they will ever learn in the boardroom. It's governance by walking around. And it's a critically important element in the search for excellent management. On top of that, staff are apt to tell a director anything. They know they're not going to get fired for revealing a problem to a director. Indeed, directors are looking for frankness.

Look for signs of problems with your culture. Beware of rapid cycling in your top team. The velocity of your turnover has implications for culture and can be a warning sign as well. Many companies permit hiring of top managers from outside and have a revolving door of people every two or three years. They are not building a culture that encourages people to stay and see the results of their efforts.

If change is frequent, the board must probe whether turnover among the top team is the result of a problem with the CEO or is a characteristic of the wider organization. Is the CEO's behavior at issue, or is the CEO a poor judge of people? Are people leaving for big promotions elsewhere? Or is the company making mistakes in firing people? To keep track, the board should ask for a monthly report of staffers who have left for other employers.

Especially in large companies, culture may not be uniform across the organization. Trian's Ed Garden, who also sits on GE's board, has found that the culture of the company varies from one line of business to another. He says, "The culture at Aviation is very different from the culture at Power. It's not homogenous. You have to go out there and touch and feel the operation."

Issues with day-to-day operations can also indicate that the culture needs to change. Culture affects operations in several critical areas, in particular the cultures of decision making, change execution, and promotions and employee development. All are mediated by the culture of interpersonal behavior. Do people engage in destructive competition? Do they hide information? Do they use abusive language? Do critical players fail to collaborate effectively? The board must ask these questions continually.

Of these elements, the culture of decision making is an overarching operational concern. What is the behavior at the nodes where big decisions are made? For example, pricing may involve several departments, with many intersections between them. To evaluate culture, probe who controls the transaction. What information and what rules are they using? What issues are they failing to confront? Is one person dominating the process? Are decisions fact-based or intuitive or a mixture of the two? If the group makes a mistake, how does it recoup? Do the people respond constructively or do they play the blame game?

The board can demand an analysis of the decision-making process and bring in external companies for an evaluation.

The board can apply the same analytical framework to the culture of promotion and advancement. The attributes of the people who win promotions—their qualities and characteristics—can reveal much about the culture. Is the process objective or not? It is not the role of the board to manage the process in any of these realms. Instead, ask for information and serve as a sounding board.

A crisis can be an opportunity to review culture. One large company that was forced to recall a product realized it had a cultural problem because different units withheld information from each other that would have let the company make better decisions. The company did not try to defend the culture. Instead, the company brought in outsiders to do an investigation and external assessment. The company followed up with a meeting to which it invited hundreds of its top leaders from around the world and asked a simple question: If they could change one thing about the company's culture, what would it be? The responses, distilled, are now part of the company's foundation.

Culture is a reflection of your talent. So to put the story of your company out into the world, tell your investors about your people. If you nurture your talent well, you will have a good story to share with your owners. Show them how your talent has a direct relationship with the creation of long-term value. The good stories shouldn't be left just to the fashion companies, whose designers are tracked by their investors, or to the pharmaceutical companies, whose investors track the R&D chief and the regulatory liaison with the Food and Drug Administration. These stories are common to all organizations. Every company should be able to tell investors how their people create value.

In the end, though, a company's culture is set at the top, often through example rather than codification. As GM's Mary Barra says, "I can't come into the office and change the culture today. But I can work on how I behave today, how I act in a meeting, how I take or don't take an action." GM has meetings with senior leaders twice a year and then quarterly calls, and most are about culture and behavior. And the board raises the topic several times a year.

The success or failure of a company will be a function of the people—their quality, their expertise, their work ethic, their culture—and how as a board you can influence them.

CHECKLIST FOR MANAGING TALENT

- Discuss talent at every board meeting.

- Determine the qualities that the CEO and the leadership team will need in the future based on strategy and marketplace trends.

- Plan ahead by identifying CEO candidates two or three layers down in the corporation.

- Use simulations to benchmark CEO candidates and put finalists through their paces in different parts of the company.

- Canvass senior colleagues and customers about all internal CEO candidates.

- Go out in the field to get to know tomorrow's likely leaders.

- Link compensation to initiatives that build future value.

- To ensure diversity in the leadership ranks, identify and nurture talent before you need it.

- To attract younger employees, adopt meaningful sustainability initiatives.

- Be on the lookout for signs of cultural problems, such as rapid turnover of top managers.

CHAPTER 2

The Strategic Imperative

I
f talent is the first pillar of the new TSR, the source of a company's strength, then strategy is the second, through which the company finds its path toward long-term growth. Talent and strategy are twinned and reciprocal: talent sets the strategy, and the strategy relies on the presence of people who have the right skills to implement it. Setting strategy and executing it well is the prime imperative of management. And oversight of strategy is thus a crucial responsibility of the board.

A principal objective of strategy is to keep the company ahead of its competitors in performance and shareholder return, both now and in the future. And an essential focus of the board's attention is the allocation of human and financial resources. In this role, the board must help management identify options, shape opportunities, and make decisions about new ventures to pursue and old ones to shed.

The new TSR demands a new approach to decision making. Most boards have used three- to five-year plans to monitor strategy. These plans might consist of a strategic agenda, details of projects, an annual budget, and a capital expenditure plan, all geared toward a target for total shareholder return.

That tool may be useful, but on its own, it is not enough. Companies today must be able to respond swiftly to volatility in the marketplace, structural uncertainty, and trends in the global economy rising to the level of existential threat.

To do so, companies must take advantage of new tools in data analytics. Indeed, if your company is not already digital at its core, it must become so or risk either total obsolescence—like Kodak, which failed to spot the shift to digital photography, and Blockbuster, which missed the trend toward streaming—or total eclipse, like Microsoft in online search, where its global market share is barely 5 percent.

Digital technology is an example of an advance whose adoption can have a profound effect on a company's ability to make money—one that standard projections of financial results might miss. For that reason, we propose that the board pay just as much attention to the company's moneymaking model as it does to strategy. A dashboard of metrics directly tied to the moneymaking model will help the board and management protect both long-term planning and short-term execution.

Customers are central to the success of strategy and the moneymaking model alike, which means that the board must learn all that it can about the company's customers and markets. Armed with that knowledge, the board can help identify new avenues of growth, just as an activist investor would.

Boards should focus on the company's moneymaking metrics and not on short-term projections of shareholder return. As they review strategy, they should be sure that it defines actions linked to moneymaking. Smart boards will span the spectrum of financial and operational concerns, concentrating on the consumer, creation of value, competitive advantage, the marketplace, talent, investors, and sustainability. We will help you tie these strands together. (See figure 2-1.)

FIGURE 2-1

The new TSR: Strategy

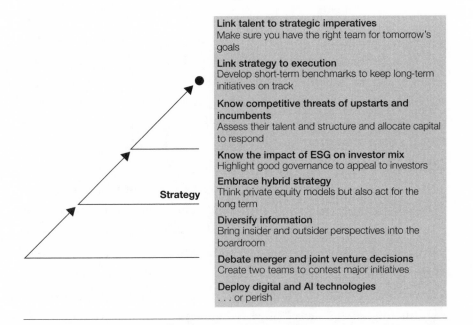

Link talent to strategic imperatives
Make sure you have the right team for tomorrow's goals

Link strategy to execution
Develop short-term benchmarks to keep long-term initiatives on track

Know competitive threats of upstarts and incumbents
Assess their talent and structure and allocate capital to respond

Know the impact of ESG on investor mix
Highlight good governance to appeal to investors

Embrace hybrid strategy
Think private equity models but also act for the long term

Diversify information
Bring insider and outsider perspectives into the boardroom

Debate merger and joint venture decisions
Create two teams to contest major initiatives

Deploy digital and AI technologies
. . . or perish

Strategy

A Moneymaking Model Linked to Strategy

In discussions of strategy, most people refer to a company's business model. The moneymaking model is different, and it can play a critical role in the creation of value in both the short and long terms.

A moneymaking model captures how the basic elements of moneymaking—such as revenue, gross margins, fixed and variable costs, and cash generation and use—combine for a particular business. Each company will have its own moneymaking model—one that might be similar to that of other companies but that will nevertheless be unique, especially in its execution.

The increasing importance of moneymaking models in the digital age was heralded by the seminal work of economist W. Brian Arthur on the science of increasing returns. His doctrine describes how the companies that get ahead in knowledge-based industries will tend to get further ahead, as opposed to the diminishing returns in smokestack industries and other legacy businesses, where successful companies slow down as they run into physical limitations.

The two sorts of businesses have different patterns of investment, earnings, and cash generation. Traditional companies build their future by making capital investments. Digital companies build theirs by hiring computer scientists and paying licensing fees, which they record as operating expenses. These expenses will suppress the earnings of the digital company, resulting in lower taxes up front, freeing up cash. Thus, digital businesses like Amazon tend to focus on cash per share, not earnings per share.

By contrast, a conventional three- to five-year plan might refer only to financial results and in so doing would not explain the interplay of the components of the moneymaking model or how well it is working. Any management review must include moneymaking metrics in addition to financial results. And it's the board's job to make sure management follows them so that the company keeps on track for long-term growth.

In the digital age, every business must reevaluate its moneymaking model. In its presentations to the board, management should elucidate the ways in which the moneymaking model is working as well as the initiatives that the company is taking to execute its plan. And when the company's financial results deviate from expectations, the board should take a hard look at its moneymaking model. Among the questions the board should periodically ask: Is the existing moneymaking model the right one, given changes in competition and technology? If not, what alternative should we consider or construct? And how would a different model affect the company's market value and other financial measures?

Execution is key to the moneymaking model—as it is to the new TSR. Talent, strategy, and risk might all be in place, but if execution breaks down, companies will stray off track. To that end, the board should create a dashboard to track milestones for initiatives and value-creating activities, and it should communicate the results to the twenty-five largest stockholders.

The board's strategic discussion must also tie together short- and long-term plans. It's the role of the board to focus management on the path to future value, with the past as a guide. When considering a new proposal, the best directors will stop to review the company's five-year strategy and ask where this venture will fit in. Implicit is a trade-off and an opportunity cost. If you're going to invest resources in a new initiative, what will you be giving up? Will you be forgoing an even better investment for the long term? The board must ask those questions.

Understanding the metrics in the moneymaking model takes time. For the board to properly oversee strategy, it must have the information and the wherewithal to evaluate it. Often boards simply don't devote as much time to strategy as they should. Rather than simply walking the board through hundred-page decks, management should have a real discussion with the directors on different strategic scenarios and how they might play out.

Management can help by distilling the information it asks the directors to digest. At GM, before the board meets, CEO Mary Barra will send the directors a two-page brief about the issues that the meeting will cover, laying out the decisions that management has made and the insights it will be seeking from the board. Challenging the team to hold the report to two pages while still touching on all of the critical points lets the company disseminate a lot of information to the board concisely and efficiently and drive discussion of strategy into every board meeting.

Getting hold of the right information will help companies see the future before their competitors, and move on from the past as well. Elena Botelho of ghSMART says, "Behind every story of a failure to adapt is actually a story of a failure to let go of something that was really profitable for a period of time but became outdated. An adaptable organization will build a business up and cannibalize it, versus Blockbuster, which could have bought Netflix for $50 million." The successful boards will ask the questions that let them anticipate what might happen tomorrow and, when necessary, turn their strategy around.

A prime example of how a moneymaking model can help companies adapt to change and create value for the long term comes from Adobe, the $11 billion maker of design software. Sales of its big-ticket packages had stalled in the wake of the 2008 financial crisis. So CEO Shantanu Narayen decided to move Adobe to a subscription service, a transformation of the company's moneymaking model.

Narayen's bet was that a large, previously untapped customer would prefer to pay a monthly, annual, or usage-based fee for access to Adobe Creative Cloud instead of a large up-front payment to own the Adobe Creative Suite package. It was a risky gambit. Adobe's customers were accustomed to outright ownership of their software and a stable product. For that reason, the board was skeptical about the new direction.

To give customers fair warning, Narayen announced the change a year in advance of its 2011 introduction and agreed to keep the two distribution models running side by side for a time. But many longtime customers did rebel, angry at the prospect of turning a onetime purchase into an annuity for Adobe. The board's doubts increased when sales dipped shortly after the subscription model debuted. But it trusted Narayen and supported him.

The benefits of the subscription model would soon become apparent, for both Adobe and many of its customers. For Adobe, the subscription model let the software maker extend its market to smaller companies and individual users. And for customers and Adobe alike, subscriptions eliminated the headache and the cost of making continual upgrades to the product after the user has installed it, necessary to keep users abreast of changing design technology. It wasn't unusual for the Creative Suite to be slightly out of date just weeks after a corporate customer had deployed it throughout its entire network.

By moving to subscriptions, Adobe changed the way it makes its money and thus the relationship between the elements of its moneymaking model. The ratio of costs to revenues declined, with gross margins and recurring revenues increasing as the cost of acquiring and retaining customers fell. If Adobe relied solely on standard financial projections to predict returns, it would never have been able to understand the benefits of the change. In fact, a company's moneymaking model, properly understood, is what makes useful financial projections possible, not the other way around.

Adobe stopped selling its Creative Suite in January 2017. By then, its stock price had more than quadrupled to $106 per share from its level at the time of Creative Cloud's launch. By September 2020, the share price had nearly quintupled again to $491—proof that understanding your moneymaking model and knowing when to change it can pay off in creating long-term value.

Modeling the Market

To support the company's moneymaking model, the board must develop its own model of the company's market and how it is evolving. The board can enlist a third party to help create this model, but the work must take place apart from management; to be independent, the board needs its own source of intelligence. As they oversee strategy, the directors should consider the model that the board has developed and compare it with management's view of the changing marketplace.

An essential component of the market model is an explicit discussion of long-term competitive advantage—its shelf life and signs of either a decline or an improvement. This analysis should be part of a measurable, analytical dashboard as well. A third party could periodically validate the assumptions underlying the competitive analysis. The board should demand these assessments from management. These measures should also be useful to management in conducting its work to create long-term shareholder return.

As you construct your market model, make good use of board members with real expertise. At GM, Barra turns to such directors to generate ideas. They are a particularly valuable resource given the transformation of the auto industry by electrification, autonomous connectivity, and other innovations. Each meeting includes a deep dive into one of those areas and draws on the collective knowledge of the board. By the time GM makes a big strategic decision—for instance, SoftBank's investment in GM Cruise and the company's partnership with Honda for self-driving cars—management has talked about it with the board multiple times and benefited from the board's insights and perspectives.

To help set strategy for the long term, some companies are taking novel steps to stay abreast of new currents in their market. Shortly before he was due to step down as CEO, Mark Turner of WSFS went on a three-month road trip to visit companies and customers in the financial services industry with the aim of learning about the market and seeking potential partnerships. He says, "I visited forty-nine different organizations across the United States and traveled more than 44,000 miles. They were traditional banks doing interesting things like Northern Trust and Huntingdon. They were traditional organizations like Walmart and Wawa and Becton Dickinson, and they were also technology companies like Google and Apple, and fintech companies in Silicon Valley and elsewhere."

An objective of the tour was to investigate megatrends that are converging on financial services. One is that millennials are overtaking boomers as the largest generation and showing fundamentally different ways of thinking and behaving. Another is the notion that big data and automated processes will remake traditional models of decision making.

But the biggest for WSFS was the inroad made by digital technology into delivery of services. Turner says, "For 187 years we had been really good at physically delivering financial services to our customers, through brick and mortar and people, augmented by systems and technology. But especially with the advent of the smartphone, more and more customers were wanting to interact with us through digital means only." The road trip helped solidify this movement. And it positioned the company to create long-term returns by adjusting its moneymaking model.

You can borrow from Turner's practice even if you stay closer to home. Boards can encourage the CEO to establish a heat-seeking

M&A or joint venture function to identify and invest in disruptive technologies or emerging companies, as Facebook did with WhatsApp, and as Amazon has done in self-driving cars.

Making Strategy Work for the Long Term

To oversee strategy, the board must first understand the senior management team behind the decisions—its biases, skills, and risk-taking profiles. Those characteristics determine the choices the team makes and the strategies it sets. In some companies, the CEO and the CFO are good dealmakers and will build the company through acquisitions. In other companies, the top managers are skilled in organic growth and have very little expertise in M&A. The board's role is to make sure they are on track with a strategy that fits their skills—or change the skills to fit the strategy.

Difficulties arise when companies stray outside the comfort zone of their leaders. The Bank of America had leaders whose strength was in organic growth, but they decided to grow via acquisitions, and two deals in 2008 killed the company—the purchases of Countrywide Financial and Merrill Lynch. Now the bank is focusing on organic growth. When anomalous behavior arises, boards need to know what advice management is getting from outside.

Keeping talent and strategy in balance is especially challenging when circumstances are changing rapidly. The sheer pace of disruption is turning a lot of businesses upside down, leading to rapid shifts in how they think about their long-term strategy. And that disruption has upended the assumptions about the people they need within the company to execute that strategy.

To help everyone stay in line, communication about strategy must flow throughout the organization. In too many companies, training is unrelated to strategic imperatives. Raj Gupta of Delphi Automotive says, "The challenge for leadership is to translate strategy to different levels inside the company, and to ensure that people connect the strategy with what they're doing." The best way is to keep everyone in the loop. Gupta has seen CEOs on a conference call with two hundred or three hundred employees at the end of the month to discuss the results during the period and the strategic imperatives and priorities for the coming month. He says, "The only way I know is constant communication and reinforcement."

With the right balance between talent and strategy, managers must focus on customers and users to execute that strategy for the long term. For its part, the board can start with good information about customers, the competition, and the marketplace so it can make sure management has what it needs. The board should have at its disposal a dashboard of indicators that capture all aspects of user experience—customer usage, behavior benefits, customer expectations, customer pain points. As part of its strategy, the company can measure the benefits to the customer today and describe how innovation will benefit customers in the future.

The board's toolbox should also include an independent survey to help determine what is unique about the company's benefits to consumers compared with the competition—and what customers will be looking for in the future. The degree to which the company meets customer needs is a critical factor in value creation, and one that activist investors focus on, too.

Some smart companies have taken steps to formalize the strategic focus on the customer. Turner of WSFS says, "For us, that was creating a chief customer experience officer to evaluate how our customers feel about interacting with us across the organization and making the appropriate changes." So far, those changes have involved creation of what the bank calls a seamless omnichannel platform—one that lets customers interact with the company in whichever way they prefer, either online or in person. Over the next several years, innovations will include seeding services using new digital tools—artificial intelligence and bots among them.

Management can help by educating their boards about their customers. CEOs might invite their boards to customer events so they can mingle with buyers and the workforce and see the products, and to investor events so they can learn how the investment community views their company in the marketplace. The company can also invite key customers to a dinner alongside board meetings. Doing so will let board members who come from different backgrounds and companies contribute by asking questions and making suggestions that draw on their strengths and insights into current trends.

The board can support a rethinking of the moneymaking model by encouraging management to align corporate strategy with digital execution. In human resources, companies can use online competitions to learn about new candidates who traditional recruitment methods might not "see." And in IT management, a company can create a new digitally enabled technology platform that can manage all employees across a range of functions and run it in parallel with its existing infrastructure. After porting over all data to the new platform, the company can then shut the old one down.

With the right people and systems in place, the board's biggest strategic role will be making decisions about major initiatives: mergers and acquisitions, divestitures, big-ticket investments, entrance into new markets, and exit from current ones. Among the prime questions that boards need to ask as they consider their strategic options is whether an initiative will be helpful or hurtful in the long term, and whether a competing technology will affect them or not. Michele Hooper of the Directors' Council says, "Let's take Blockbuster or Redbox back in the day. I bet they wish they had more people in their boardroom who were naysayers about the fact that their CDs, videos, eight-track tapes, or whatever the heck they used to sell or rent were not going to be long for the world because streaming was going to become a thing." Too many people in the boardroom, and too many people in management, simply couldn't see what was coming.

With such disasters in mind, do your best when setting your plans to anticipate the early warning signs of failure. That forethought can help you select the strategies you're best able to handle for the long term. Often the simple questions are the ones that get people thinking in a contrarian way. A course of action might seem to be the obvious choice. But a lot is at stake, so try to find the things that would make the choice just as obviously wrong.

Encourage management to consider all strategic possibilities and to think in terms of generating options, not just an answer. Doing so changes the game. When you look at options, you can debate them. And then you have permitted the board members to engage in an open discussion and bring their own perspective.

Challenging your ideas can also help you winnow out confirmation bias and identify flaws in your thinking. People often claim to have unbiased opinions. Usually they don't. Instead they spend their intellectual energy looking for arguments that support their premise, whether to do a deal or prove the benefits of a new strategy. Having an impartial person bring a fresh pair of eyes to an idea can reveal not only its benefits but also the alternatives and the risks.

This sort of engagement will help create a strategy more effectively than simply presenting a plan. In the end, it's better for management if the board is a partner, not an approver. The practice of considering all strategic options should apply to every competitive initiative, from product launches to mergers and acquisitions.

Of these, the most fraught—because they are the most far-reaching and usually the most expensive—are mergers and acquisitions. Whenever the company is planning a merger, the board should propose bringing in an opposing point of view. Former T. Rowe Price chair and United Technologies board member Brian Rogers helped UT through such a process when it was thinking about buying Rockwell Collins.

Aside from questioning the economics and strategic basis of the deal, the board's role was to ask if the company has the organizational talent to pull it off. Rogers says, "The job was to challenge management strategy and the economics of a hypothetical transaction. So we brought in what I call a deal assassin to shoot holes through the Rockwell Collins acquisition."

The starting premise for such a review is to make sure that the company won't be fixing something that isn't broken. If your company is performing well and has a good culture, why would you contemplate an acquisition? What would be a fair price, and a price that investors would accept? What would be a price that would hurt shareholders? Rogers adds, "This was probably the first time we brought in someone to take potshots at both the rationale and the organizational issues and also the price. It's a practice that makes a lot of sense." United Technologies completed the acquisition in 2018.

A variation on the theme of the deal assassin is the premerger bake-off. The concept is not new but often misapplied. For instance, many companies planning an acquisition will bring in two investment bankers to make presentations about how they would structure a deal. The banker that offers the best package will get the job. But bankers only get their fee if a merger takes place, which puts pressure on both teams to build momentum for a deal, whether it is good for the company or not.

Warren Buffett, chair of Berkshire Hathaway, has turned the process on its head. He reports that one of his companies was particularly unsuccessful at M&As, but its basic business was so good that it could just keep doing them. So he took steps to protect the company from its worst impulses. He told the board to make it a fair fight by bringing in two investment bankers—one who presents the case for the deal and one who presents the case against it. And the one who wins the case and makes the recommendation that the board accepts will get a larger payment. That process eliminates the incentive for both bankers to sell the deal.

Such analysis can also help you make decisions about what you could divest in the interest of long-term growth. As part of its oversight, the board should continually be questioning management about its portfolio to ensure it is bringing the right products to market. Raj Gupta of Delphi Automotive says, "Complexity is the enemy of cost and speed and causes a suboptimal capital allocation every single time. If you have a focused portfolio and a significant market position, everyone from the board to the lowest person in the organization will really understand what we are trying to do in each business." More than three markets are too many. Simplifying the portfolio and focusing it should be part of an important strategic discussion.

Knowing your strengths can help you make the hard choices about what to sell and when to sell it. Rohm & Haas was well known for manufacturing Plexiglas and was the first company to develop a synthetic fungicide. Both product lines were moneymakers and part of the company's heritage. But they were becoming commodities, and Rohm & Haas was not great at selling commodity products. So the company decided to get out of those businesses. Despite their profitability, they were too small and were not going to be part of the company's future. A lot of emotions were swirling around that decision, according to Gupta, who was CEO of Rohm & Haas at the time. But he calls the change one of the best things that the company did.

A Strategically Correct Acquisition

The right acquisition, impelled by a focus on the processes that enable long-term growth, can help transform an old-line company into a new-line one. Perhaps the prime example of a corporation that has made such a metamorphosis, and with stellar results, is Danaher Corp.

Danaher was founded in 1984 by Steven and Mitchell Rales as a diversified manufacturer. The brothers quickly acquired more than a dozen companies in a range of tool and instrumentation businesses. One of these, Jacobs Manufacturing Co., a maker of pneumatic braking systems for trucks (earning it the moniker Jake's Brakes), was struggling to improve its profit margin. The Rales brothers knew that Toyota was adept at expanding margins, so they sent a team to Japan to learn how Toyota did it.

Toyota's method has three parts: setting a high bar for growth, with ambitious targets across the range of company operations; adopting best practices in the industry and spreading them throughout the corporation—not just to the manufacturing arm, say, but to the sales force, too; and inculcating a culture of continuous improvement, so as not to be satisfied with current margins even if they are better than the industry average. Raj Ratnakar, former head of strategy at Danaher and now chief strategy officer at DuPont, recalls, "The brothers told me, 'Raj, we're going to teach you to be greedy. You should never be satisfied.' It's a skill, and an art, and a cultural religion."

In 2015, Danaher made its big pivot. Over the years, the company had added life sciences businesses to its manufacturing portfolio. Danaher decided to spin out its traditional industrial units and refocus the company on biopharma systems. As part of this change, Danaher set its sights on Pall, a filtration company. Filtration is essential in the manufacture of biologic drugs, yet biopharma filtration represented only 30 percent of Pall's revenues. So buying Pall would mean paying a huge premium over the value of the part of the business that the company actually wanted, like buying a house so you can use the swimming pool.

The decision came down to CEO Tom Joyce and the board. When Joyce is considering an acquisition, he doesn't set up a bake-off like Buffett does. Instead, he serves as a one-man army of opposition and forces the deal backers to make him say yes. "He's a grinch," says Ratnakar. "He won't give you a dime until you prove your point." He would even call industry colleagues in the middle of a meeting to bounce his team's ideas off them.

The board has a similarly sharp focus, challenging management to make the right judgment in the way that a private equity firm would. It has built the company with that image in mind. To help Danaher respond swiftly, the board has kept the company stripped down, removing bureaucracy whenever it makes an acquisition. In meetings, the board wants data. "There's no time to be nice to anybody," says Ratnakar. "If you go in with charts and pretty pictures, you'll get creamed. But instead of flying arrows, you'll have a rich discussion. You work hard, and after the meeting you come out sweating."

Unlike most private equity firms, Danaher has a long time horizon, giving it the best of both worlds—focus and time. Whenever you pay top price for an asset, you always run the risk of falling flat on your face. So Ratnakar and his team conducted a deep review of the market, not only taking a static view of where the industry was at the time but using analytical tools that let them map out the market landscape to predict coming trends.

Supported by their review, the team convinced the board that Pall would help Danaher become a major player in biopharma systems, and that the acquisition would pay off despite the high price tag. The deal closed in 2015 for $13.8 billion. It has proven to be a linchpin of Danaher's transformation and a key to its long-term growth. In the five years from October 2015 to October 2020, the company's share price tripled. And over the past thirty years, Danaher has earned the greatest return of any diversified manufacturing company save Roper, showing that if boards are willing to follow the precepts of the new TSR, their total return can be spectacular.

Strategic Initiatives

Acquisitions aren't the only decisions that demand sharp strategic focus. For instance, you can apply the Buffett plan to any of your big strategic initiatives and red-team them as well. Mary Erdoes of J.P. Morgan Asset & Wealth Management extends the model to new product reviews. On one side of the table, she'll set up the backers of a new product. On the other side will be the opponents who will give all the reasons the product won't work—it's not the right time or the right audience. By encouraging the formation of red and blue teams to debate the merits of a proposal, the board can help the company disrupt itself and move to a better model for the future.

Indeed, whenever you are considering an important change of any sort, we recommend running a contest between the strategy and its direct countermeasure—two viable but mutually exclusive strategic options. Management would generate the options and discuss them with the board. And the board can ask a third party to come in to discuss which of the strategies it would recommend based on outside information.

Some smart companies get that intelligence from competitors. While he was on the Silicon Valley leg of his tour, Turner of WSFS visited fintech companies that were purposefully trying to transform the financial services industry. Yet because of the tight regulation in the business, these players were not going to be able to fully disrupt what the banks did. That barrier presented an opportunity. Turner says, "They were going to be good partners over the long term. We both had strengths, and they were complementary. Banks had lots of customers. We had brand, we had trust, we had regulatory know-how. They had younger, more aggressive talent and a lot of new ideas. They weren't hampered by legacy systems and thinking."

Until then, WSFS had grown through small acquisitions, like bolt-ons. After Turner returned, the company used what he learned from the tour to make the largest acquisition in its history, Beneficial Bank, which doubled the size of the company and helped it expand into digital services by giving it a strong presence in online and mobile banking. WSFS viewed the assimilation of Beneficial not just as a traditional cost-cutting exercise—how to take out redundant expenses while keeping all the customers—but also as an opportunity to transform the company.

Strategy Performance Evaluation

To make sure strategy is on track for the long term, boards must continually evaluate performance. And that is especially true of big-ticket initiatives. For instance, after any acquisition, the board should conduct a postmortem. Warren Buffett says, "I was at a company that made about eight acquisitions, none of which worked out, and they could hardly wait to do the ninth. So I suggested that we have a postmortem just like a hospital on every acquisition two or three years later and objectively decide—not with recriminations or anything—just what actually did happen."

If your merger turned out to be a bad one, learn why, and your next deal will be better. At least once a year, many of the boards on which Michele Hooper of the Directors' Council sits will go through every deal from the past three years and review the premise in the capital request and the strategic plan for each transaction. By reflecting on the problems they had to fix in deals, good companies can become great at making acquisitions.

Follow the same process for other big initiatives. Look back to see if the economics of a strategic decision paid off. The board should assess whether an initiative achieved its financial goals, whether the expected synergies materialized, whether the company retained its clients—in other words, whether the company accomplished strategically what it set out to do. If a venture goes off the rails, the question is whether you can pick up the path in your original plan or if the idea is one you're going to end up regretting. In that case, the board must figure out what went wrong and why—the company either was overly ambitious and neglected to take important intermediate steps or didn't move quickly enough.

Boards must be bold enough to probe management about anomalies in strategic performance. Don't be afraid to ask "Why?" Sometimes the drivers of performance—both good and bad—are not obvious. Ron O'Hanley of State Street says, "Having the benefit of everything that's been published about Wells Fargo, it does seem there were some early warning signs that the board missed. Firing five thousand people for anything strikes me as, why didn't the antenna go up there?"

Boards should question positive news, too. After a blowout year or two or three, boards need the discipline to probe whether things are a little too good to be true. At root is the importance of understanding the basis of a company's strength or weakness. The best boards will question management on competitive advantage. They will ask what they will do if their advantage goes away or the classic Amazon or Google disruptor comes in.

Throughout, remember that the board is there to oversee the company, not to run it. The board must find the right balance in the level and the depth of its strategic oversight. Things that go awry may be the result of a great strategy poorly executed. That possibility presents the board with the dilemma of deciding where governance ends and management begins. As former Vanguard CEO Jack Brennan says, "The gap between the two should be really wide. It's a problem when a director gets confused as to which is which."

A Strategy for All Stakeholders

The sustainability of global economic activity is likely to be the defining issue of the coming generation. For that reason, the varied initiatives that encompass corporate social responsibility have changed from charitable activities to essential ones.

Shareholders occupy a hybrid niche in the business ecosystem. They are buyers—customers—who might have entrusted their retirement income and life savings to the care of an investment management company. But, as the three of us have often said, along with many of the people we interviewed for this book, the shareholders are also the owners. As such, they own a share of the ethical responsibility for the consequences of the economic activities from which their profits derive. And since their ownership is diffuse, giving them no direct control over management decisions, it falls to the board to make sure that the ethical responsibilities of the shareholders are met.

And those responsibilities are manifest. Any discussion of sustainability involves a consideration of shareholder value versus the public good. This era fundamentally alters that relationship. Until now, one could argue that maximizing shareholder value was ultimately in the public interest, because an increase would benefit shareholders directly and could also benefit everyone else through whatever redistributive mechanisms a government chose to implement.

The growing climate emergency changes that equation. For the first time, we have measurable, actionable evidence that a goal primarily fixed on an acceleration of economic activity might not contribute to the public good and could even lead to catastrophe. Collectively, people have not been good stewards of the world's resources. Those chickens are coming home to roost. Shareholders must take note as companies do.

As a consequence, some investment firms, including BlackRock, the world's largest fund manager, are divesting fossil fuel companies from their actively traded funds. BlackRock says it is doing so in the public interest, but CEO Larry Fink has said that an earlier move to divest stocks of companies that manufacture guns helped the bottom line.

Why might that be so? If companies that adopt sustainability goals do well by attracting millennial employees and investors, then all things being equal, those companies should gain competitive advantage versus peers that don't adopt such goals. Fund managers that exclude the latter class of companies from their funds should do well by their own investors, too.

Companies still have to deliver relative to their competition; you might not have the best returns, but you cannot have the worst. Former Xerox CEO Anne Mulcahy says, "As a company we have a responsibility to provide shareholders with a fair return. But sustainability is one of the pillars of corporate responsibility. These [measures] should not be challenged as a misuse of bottom-line business returns. I do think that the best businesses comprehend those values."

Such considerations are especially relevant today. The question of whether to implement sustainability initiatives—as energy companies, including BP, have pledged to meet net-zero carbon goals and financial services companies have made divestment decisions—will inevitably involve more than the effect on the bottom line.

Increasingly, companies have stopped looking at sustainability measures as charitable work. Shelly Lazarus, former CEO of Ogilvy & Mather, says,

When it started, it was in the philanthropic, societal do-good, we're-meeting-our-obligations-as-good-corporate-citizens bucket. It's now part of how the best companies are run because it's becoming increasingly important to all the constituents of any company. If you're market driven, the market has spoken about whether these things are important or not—how you treat your resources, how you interact with the community, how long term you are in your thinking about your impact on society.

Indeed, long-term planning and sustainability measures are mutually reinforcing. Long-term planning is a necessary condition for sustainability initiatives, which is a long-term issue if there ever was one. But the reverse is true as well. Sustainability can be the imperative that short-circuits short-term thinking—the rationale that justifies looking beyond short-term goals such as boosting share price.

Companies address climate change out of concern for potential catastrophe in their businesses, too. The most obvious example is what Coca-Cola would do if we run out of water. It is a board-level discussion. The company now has programs designed to promote water sustainability. Yes, for the sake of the wider society, sustainability must be a primary consideration in all strategic decisions, but in this case sustainability of the company, too, is contingent on having adequate water supplies in the future. If we all keep going in the current direction, we may not.

So there is an inextricable link between the interests of your customers, your employees, and society and the creation of long-term value. The real dichotomy is not between stakeholder capitalism and shareholder capitalism. We don't think there needs to be a difference between the two when you are thinking about the long term. That is, in the long term, taking care of stakeholders can lead to better long-term shareholder value.

This notion has the support of some activist investors. Jeffrey Ubben, founder of the hedge fund ValueAct Capital and a new hedge fund, Inclusive Capital Partners, says, "Sustainability is a solve for short-termism." He recommends moving CEO compensation to terms of five or more years because "you need to protect the CEO and allow him [sic] to talk to boards about sustainability as a way to combat short-termism."

But Ubben didn't think traditional investment firms were going far enough to support long-term value creation. In 2020, he cofounded Inclusive Capital Partners to focus on environmental and social impact investments as a way to boost value at old-line corporations, telling one newspaper that he's going to have to find new shareholders who want to be focused on the long term, and expressing doubts that investment companies can do a good job of running both traditional funds and impact ones.

Ultimately, though, measuring long-term financial returns of sustainability initiatives is impossible. Dan Riff of Advantage Solutions says, "The idea that you'd ask Walmart to estimate a return on their investment of sending [crops] to help people in Houston or Florida after their hurricanes feels inconsistent with the spirit in which those investments were made. It always ties back to the three- and five-year performance of the company, but pushing companies to precisely measure the returns on individual investments in these areas is a slippery slope, and I'm not an advocate."

The message seems to be that while sustainability measures should be good for the bottom line, they mustn't be dismissed if they aren't. Boards should be under no illusion: acting in the social good will sometimes mean leaving money on the table. But employees and investors are questioning companies because as individuals they are making decisions about the sort of company they wish to work for and invest in. Those questions are forcing companies to make decisions about the sort of organization they wish to be. And since a company is its talent, those same questions are forcing managers and directors to decide what sort of people they wish to be, too.

If you're not convinced that sustainability measures will help boost total shareholder return for your company, or you're tempted to appeal to stakeholders with measures that amount to little more than greenwashing—designed to look good without costing very much—then consider the biblical argument. There's a moral imperative to support climate initiatives even if they cost you money—and if you disobey the moral imperative, it all ends in the apocalypse. We're not talking only about the apocalypse that might come upon the world if we haven't achieved net-zero carbon emissions by 2050, as the Paris Agreement holds, but the legislative one that may well occur quite a bit sooner.

For young people today, the world is extremely fragile, and the fragility is not theoretical. Most of the people working on this book will be offstage by 2050; environmental activist Greta Thunberg and her generation will be in early middle age. And for them, the coronavirus pandemic has been a dress rehearsal, the calamity that proves their point and shows that the hard work necessary to forestall disaster is doable.

Think how quickly the world reacted to the pandemic—shutting down theaters, museums, cinemas, and restaurants, and then schools and places of employment; closing borders to travelers; locking down the populace—all in a matter of weeks. We've seen how quickly people and governments around the world can act when they attack a problem with urgency. We can expect large swaths of society to address climate change with equal urgency—to say that 2050 is too long to wait, that we must do more and do it more quickly.

Our recommendation to companies: get out in front of the issue. Every public company should pledge to undertake immediate, meaningful, verifiable actions to achieve net-zero emissions by 2050. And every public company should support federal legislation requiring such action by all so there will be no first-actor penalties.

In so doing, you will be aligning your company's strategic mindset, goals, and vision with the interests of your longest-term shareholders, which stretch far beyond the tenure of the directors or the CEO or the CEO's successor. Imagine the twenty-five-year-old employees who invested in your stock with the hopes of retiring in forty years. You are stewards for their assets. Consider them when setting your company's time horizon.

In the long run, it will all be to the good.

CHECKLIST FOR MANAGING STRATEGY

- Create a dashboard of metrics to track milestones for initiatives that create long-term value.

- Use strategic discussions in the boardroom to tie together short- and long-term plans.

- Use board members with special expertise to create your model for long-term growth.

- Send managers on the road to keep abreast of new currents in their business.

- Encourage the CEO to identify and invest in disruptive technologies and emerging companies.

- When contemplating a merger or a big strategic initiative, bring in an opposing viewpoint or stage a bake-off between teams for it and against it.

- Do a postmortem every year to track whether mergers have performed as projected.

- Periodically review which businesses play to your strengths and long-term objectives to help make hard choices about what to divest.

- Probe managers about anomalies in strategic performance, both positive and negative.

- Consider the needs of all stakeholders as a way to help build shareholder return for the long term.

CHAPTER 3

Managing Risk

The great recession. The Boeing disaster. Covid-19. The early-warning systems of America's corporations have failed them in recent years, not only because companies did not foresee disastrous events but also because they weren't prepared to act when unknown risks came upon them. Nor were they ready to manage the long-term opportunities that risk can present.

Risk is the third pillar of the new TSR, against which boards assess strategy. And changing the way they think about risk is one of the mandates for boards in managing for the long term. Traditionally, boards have focused on financial risk to minimize the chance of loss. Certainly in an era where parlous threats can arrive at any moment, mitigation of this sort of risk can be the board's most sobering responsibility. But the prime objective of the new TSR is creation of future value. That goal requires boards to reconceive their notion of risk.

Boards that embrace the new TSR will need to confront two different but related facets of risk. The board must plan for the possibility that events may arise that result in calamity—the risk that could be fatal. Some of these risks we know but cannot assign a probability to, like cybercrime; we might have ideas for how to forestall or mitigate that risk. Other risks come like a bolt from the blue, like Covid-19, leaving us at a collective loss for how to proceed.

At the same time, a key question in the management of risk—in knowing how to monitor risk and make decisions about it—is the risk appetite of the board. This facet of risk represents the potential to grow. Business is not just about making money from continuing operations. Business entails risk at its core. Risk represents an opportunity to make the intelligent, informed bets necessary for long-term growth. Companies need to be able to manage that risk to take advantage of those opportunities in all circumstances.

You will never be able to predict the unknowable. But we can show you what mechanisms you can put in place to protect your company if an unanticipated threat arises. And we can help you decide what level of risk is worth accepting so that your company can survive, and flourish, for the long term. (See figure 3-1.)

Immediate Risks

The spectrum of risk—its sources, its impact, its causes, its threats—is ever expanding. Some risks are companywide; some affect specific lines of business. Risks might originate outside the company or arise from within. We will show you how smart companies respond to risk from all sources.

Every year, the board should set the priorities for dealing with the most immediate risks confronting the company. Of the emergent risks that are today threatening the ability to achieve long-term growth, these are the most pressing:

Macroeconomic and geopolitical risk. The trend toward insular, more protectionist activity is real. Trump and Brexit were the two most

FIGURE 3-1

The new TSR: Risk

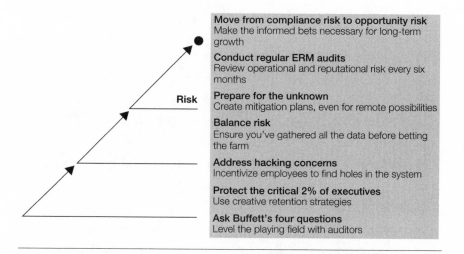

Risk

Move from compliance risk to opportunity risk
Make the informed bets necessary for long-term growth

Conduct regular ERM audits
Review operational and reputational risk every six months

Prepare for the unknown
Create mitigation plans, even for remote possibilities

Balance risk
Ensure you've gathered all the data before betting the farm

Address hacking concerns
Incentivize employees to find holes in the system

Protect the critical 2% of executives
Use creative retention strategies

Ask Buffett's four questions
Level the playing field with auditors

obvious cases in recent years, but directors must deal with the likelihood that globalization is in retreat, for good or ill.

Cybersecurity risk. It's not just about losing proprietary information. It's about losing customer loyalty—potentially forever. Very few directors understand the vulnerabilities, let alone how to protect their company against a hack.

Activism risk. The tension between long-term and short-term strategies has never been greater. Companies are pincered between the threat to company integration posed by short-term activists and the constant pressure on management from long-term activists.

Risk of individual bad actors. Sexual harassment, financial or technology theft, fraud—individual bad actors can leave the company facing billions in losses from fines and lost customers, as Volkswagen faced in the aftermath of its diesel emissions scandal, and long-term damage to a company's reputation, values, and principles, as at Wells Fargo and Boeing.

Supply-chain risk. Many companies have pushed just-in-time delivery to hold down inventory costs and respond nimbly to demand. As we are seeing in the wake of the coronavirus pandemic, companies can no longer count on uninterrupted access to their suppliers.

Here is how to move forward.

Do You Have the Resources to Survive?

The pandemic exposed what every company should have known: to ensure its long-term prospects, it must have a plan for the worst-case scenario at the ready. The more liquidity your company has, the more options you will have to move through a crisis. The companies that have managed responsible balance sheets—sometimes to the dismay of short-term investors—are best positioned to survive and flourish. As Korn Ferry CEO Gary Burnison says, "The worst-case scenarios now must be viewed as the base case."

To position themselves for long-term survival, companies must be ready to eliminate all unnecessary expenses and to rejustify all others. Former Con-way CEO Doug Stotlar, a director at AECOM, LSC Communications, and Reliance Steel & Aluminum, says that among the actions companies need to consider are a review of all planned capital expenditures; the drawing down of credit lines to create a quarantined account for emergency liquidity; temporary reductions in senior management salaries of 10 percent to 20 percent, depending on seniority, with comparable cuts taken by the board; and balancing the pace of accounts receivable with accounts payable.

In many boardrooms, directors are encouraging management teams to work more closely with their bankers. All items must be on the table, including debt strategies and options for financing and refinancing. Focus all your plans on cash preservation.

Having the right expertise will help you respond more quickly. Estée Lauder presiding director Irv Hockaday, who served as lead director at

Ford during the financial crisis, credits John Thornton, a fellow Ford director and a former co-CEO of Goldman Sachs, with being instrumental in Ford's survival of its liquidity crisis owing to his reputation in the banking community. If you want to protect yourself in the long term as you navigate the new corporate realities, make sure your boardroom has someone who commands respect in the financial world.

Talent Risk

If a company is its people, it must treat the risk of losing talent as a critical factor in its ability to realize its long-term goals. In planning for this risk, the board must choose between two disparate strategies. The first is to avoid risk by investing extra money to prevent talent from leaving. To do so, you should calculate the sum necessary to invest in retention bonuses for critical staff in order to lock up your talent pool for a certain number of years. The second is risk acceptance. You would recognize that a certain number of critical staff might leave in the absence of special inducements and gain the advantage of having extra money to invest in other initiatives.

The board's role in this choice is to ensure that management gathers the information necessary to make a logical decision about its approach. That is, management would have to demonstrate how much the company would need to invest to curtail talent loss versus how much long-term value the company might create with the same investment elsewhere, knowing that loss of talent itself has clear implications for the creation of long-term value. In this regard, Roger Ferguson, CEO of TIAA, argues that boards must expand their conception of risk beyond traditional concerns of audit and liquidity. He says, "Better board knowledge of talent and strategy and culture helps with risk mitigation and risk as an opportunity."

This discussion is essential in the post-pandemic era because leadership continuity during a crisis is crucial. Ron Williams, the former CEO of Aetna and a director of Johnson & Johnson, American Express, and Boeing, reminds us that companies need an emergency succession plan for all key executives—not just the CEO and CFO. Indeed, to position your company for the long term, you must take steps to identify and protect the people responsible for your critical capabilities.

One rule of thumb we like is that 2 percent of the people in your company are responsible for managing 98 percent of its value. For companies that make things, the sources of supply and manufacturing facilities are critical capabilities. Tim Richmond, executive vice president and head of human resources at pharmaceutical maker AbbVie, says, "Different levels of capability create different levels of risk. Identifying and separating them helps us allocate resources efficiently."

To reduce the risk of losing key people, the board must understand the risks associated with each of the company's critical capabilities. Richmond points out, for example, that for pharmaceutical companies, arranging for market access for each drug is a crucial task, involving negotiations with governments so that the company can place its products. He says, "Directors who are not from the pharmaceuticals industry wouldn't know this. Boards should take the time to understand the unique characteristics of your company that will be differentiating factors between being a good company and a great company or even a viable company." More to the point here, who is responsible for accomplishing these tasks? If the board ignores these factors, it opens the company to the risk of missing the market.

Mergers also present companies with a talent risk that few companies consider beyond short-term retention agreements for C-suite executives. Yet the depth of talent of the company you are buying will be a critical factor in the long-term success of the larger entity.

As a consequence, boards should demand a human capital audit before all mergers. Companies will typically pore over the debt and balance sheet of a target company, do a legal scrub to identify outstanding issues, and conduct a strategic risk analysis to make sure the pieces fit together. But very few companies size up the quality of the entire management team and the likelihood that the team will stay intact once the deal is done.

For instance, most company leaders don't stick around very long after a merger. Change of control provisions kick in, allowing leaders to get rich quickly and cash out. The old CEO often feels hemmed in and defanged by having to report to the new one. And the surviving company has an incentive to let the old team go because the buyer will want to take costs out. So before closing a deal, do an audit of the top twenty-five people to get a sense of how many will stay so you can have a clear idea of what you're actually buying. Companies usually conduct these audits after the merger is completed, and then it is too late.

Strategic Risk

Managing strategy involves the same trade-off between risk avoidance and risk acceptance. Risk acceptance appears most obviously in financial measures—the amount of liquidity maintained, the debt-to-capital ratio, the duration of bonds. In financial institutions, these measures are very tightly regulated and controlled. The Federal Reserve, for instance, dictates necessary levels of capital on hand. These financial institutions also create opportunities to make money through risk arbitrage, but activities in this sphere are also regulated.

At nonfinancial institutions, decisions about strategic risk opportunity are the province of the board, with the market providing effective regulation of the risk, as through the floating of junk bonds. Companies also demonstrate acceptance of risk through M&A activities, where a CEO might make a final bid and express a decision to go no further, which the board might overrule and give the OK to proceed.

How does this play out in the world? Catalent, a $3.1 billion pharmaceutical services company, provides a fine example. In 2017, after CEO John Chiminski and the board decided to pursue a more aggressive growth strategy, Chiminski began searching for acquisitions that would position the company in faster-growing segments of the market. He found Cook Pharmica, a contract manufacturer of biologics, which he thought would be a good fit for Catalent. He made an offer, with the board's backing, but the seller was holding out for a higher price. After a few rounds of back-and-forth, Chiminski was ready to give up. His board, however, was more interested in the value that the deal was likely to create than in the price and encouraged Chiminski to bid higher. That focus on the balance between risk and reward helped Chiminski get past his caution. He would go on to make what turned out to be a game-changing acquisition for $950 million, boosting Catalent's market value from $6 billion before the deal closed in 2017 to $20 billion by late 2020.

Sometimes it is the board that has a conservative bent. Directors may be reluctant to support an acquisition or major expansion that the CEO sees as a great opportunity. Here, the CEO should take the time to lay out the facts and the rationale for proceeding.

In such cases, as with the Catalent deal, at issue is a difference of opinion on the value of risk opportunity and the benefits of embracing risk. These are major projects in which a gamble will put a lot of debt on the company. Either the decision maker will look good or the deal will leave the company unmoored. So embracing risk opportunity can lead to financial risk, business risk, and microeconomic risk—including the risk of companies or their customers going under, as in the early 1990s, when Citigroup's loans for leveraged buyouts, the developing world, and real estate all defaulted. Throughout, boards must be conscious of their own risk-reward biases and those of the CEO.

Taking on such risks is a key strategic decision. In many companies, risk is the purview of the audit committee, but this body is not suited for overseeing nonfinancial risk. We believe that the primary role in managing these risks should belong to the strategy and risk committee, and shows why we like to combine the two functions in one place. The committee should own these decisions and be responsible for them.

But your board may not have the people you need to do that job. You may have several directors qualified to chair the audit committee, but they are likely to be adept mainly in the domains of accounting policy and financial reporting. You may find that you have a shortage of people in technology and tech risk management to fill the board slots you need. (For more on the subject, see chapter 5.) If your board doesn't have a risk committee, your audit committee should engage outside experts. Many organizations can serve in this function for a fee. Make sure that you're covered.

Even more to the point, the audit function addresses only one element of risk—the risk you want to mitigate, not the sort you might embrace and profit from. Mark Turner, former CEO of WSFS Financial, says, "The audit committee is not a risk management committee. It's a risk avoidance committee. Organizations make a mistake unless they are able to separate those mindsets in that committee." And whichever committee has primary responsibility for risk, it must spread its intelligence to all the directors. Turner adds, "Everybody on the board needs to understand what our risk appetites are, what our risk measurements are, what our key risk indicators are, how we manage risk, and where we're falling down."

If the essence of business is the willingness to accept risk, all too often boards are the problem, with implications not only for individual companies but for the long-term survival of the public markets. Boards are not paid to take risks. In fact, they push the CEO not to take risks; the board of Catalent was an outlier. Jeffrey Ubben of ValueAct Capital and Inclusive Capital says, "Boards are usually not ones to take contrarian activities. They are usually informed by what's coming through the lens of the CEO and management team. They are afraid to take near-term hits to the business, and afraid to push back on the CEO." If directors fold too quickly, it's because they prefer to take the path of least resistance.

As a result, Ubben believes that the public markets are dying, and private markets are probably mispriced, with expected returns too low. He says, "All the wealth is going to accrue to private owners. It is going to widen the economic income disparity."

Companies that tend to be conservative also play to short-termism. Because they don't take many chances, they're not looking at the opportunity that risk presents, leaving themselves vulnerable to disruptors. Such was the risk that upended the newspaper business, where the real risk turned out to be that customers would get content for free elsewhere. The possibility that your entire business could be disrupted means that playing it safe and sticking to the status quo for too long can be the riskiest course of all. The people trying to take the least risk become the ones taking the greatest.

It's a course that guarantees eventual obsolescence. As Elena Botelho of ghSMART says, "Behind every story of failure to adapt is actually a story of failure to let go of something that was really profitable for a period of time but became outdated."

Disruption can arise from within a company as well. Any time a business goes through a significant transition, it raises its risk profile. It might have had steady growth and stable competition, and all of its business processes in place. Then it makes an acquisition, and everything changes. It has disrupted itself. But of the two forms of disruption, this path is the better one, because you have the chance to plan for change and manage its effects for long-term value.

Disruption risk is an example of how risk response is becoming more important than risk prevention. As hard as you may try to spot potential risk, a lot of the time you will be surprised. The ability to change direction and respond to risk quickly and effectively is just as important as identifying it. To do so, you must anticipate the risk of events that can affect the entire company, and you must conceive of your company as a single organism.

Total Enterprise Risk

Managing risk in the post-pandemic era necessitates consideration of factors that threaten not only the ability to create long-term value but also your company's survival. The role of the board must be to ensure that the company has a system for identifying outlying threats and a process for responding to them. Providing substance to any legislation passed in the wake of an emergency would be a survey of every major company, with each asked to identify best practices for risk control, look for common issues, and perhaps share data in liaison with govern-ment. Staff under the CEO and general counsel can manage this early warning system.

The goal would be to construct a model for total enterprise risk—that is, risk affecting the operation of the company as a whole. At Tyco International, a major maker of components for the auto industry, the value of a companywide risk-assessment system came to the fore during the 2009 outbreak of the H1N1 swine flu epidemic. The virus appeared in Mexico, where the company had manufacturing facilities, in April of that year, confronting Tyco with a decision about whether to close its plants. Doing so could pose the possibility that its customers would face severe penalties for defaulting on contracts with automakers.

Tyco had implemented a system of enterprise risk management (ERM) in the wake of the financial fraud of its previous CEO, Dennis Kozlowski. The first step was to identify a dozen or so risk categories affecting the entire company. Initially these categories included finan-cial, legal, strategy, environmental, and intellectual property risks, and they would change every year. Members of Tyco's ERM committee each took responsibility for one risk area, with each pulling together a companywide team and informing the board about their findings periodically.

Management then assessed risks in its ten largest business units to find risk categories that were specific to each one and did the same to identify risks particular to each geographic region. Thus, Tyco's system both cut across the entire company and burrowed down into the indi-vidual businesses.

That system was crucial in helping the company respond to the swine flu crisis. Before, individual lines of business operated independ-ently of each other and without much reference to how their opera-tions affected the company's overall performance. Those concerns were front and center in 2009. The ERM assessment committee convinced the business unit team leaders to conduct their own vigorous risk as-sessments by showing them how the closing of a components plant in Mexico would compel other plants that used the components to close as well. The committee also won support from corporate with a forceful presentation of these knock-on effects. By having its ERM system up and running, Tyco was able to respond swiftly to the crisis.

Though Tyco was looking at risk broadly, you cannot make broad generalizations about risk. Ron O'Hanley, CEO of State Street, says, "The quality and breadth of enterprise risk varies dramatically both across industries and even within industries and sectors across companies." So how should your board think about risk? You should lift up your eyes and look out over the horizon for at least five to ten years. The longer the time horizon, the wider you must cast your net to encompass all possibilities. For instance, for climate risk, you must accept that more things can happen than will happen, and that you must prepare for all of them.

Directors who sit on the boards of multiple companies can give good insight into the different ways total enterprise risk can play out in different settings. Former T. Rowe Price chair Brian Rogers has served on the boards of both United Technologies (now Raytheon) and Lowe's. At United Technologies, the principal concern is product risk. He says, "I think of products that go into the global airline fleet and of cybersecurity risk in the electronics in the plane cockpit. The big risks at Lowe's are that the website goes down on Black Friday, which, in fact, it did last fall, resulting in a significant loss of revenue, at least temporarily. I don't really worry an awful lot about Lowe's products the way I worry about UTC's products."

One way to help manage total enterprise risk is to construct a risk matrix—companywide versus business-specific risks, and risks generated outside the company versus those arising internally. For each sort of risk, you must decide how to identify and then how to respond to it—that is, whether to mitigate the risk or take advantage it of by creating long-term opportunities.

A matrix would help you see both horizontal and vertical risk. Delphi Automotive chair Raj Gupta takes such a two-tier approach. The first tier is top-down risk—the overarching, enterprise-level risks that will affect any of the company's operations in the long term, such as location of assets in a highly challenged geographic region or transformative forces in your industry or currency and other economic risks. The second tier consists of what Gupta calls inside-out risks—the risks in each part of the business. They might be a manufacturing problem or the challenges of integrating a big acquisition. The trick is tying the two together—how the interrelationship of risks between different units can affect the entire company.

Just identifying risks is not sufficient. You also have to think about the probability of occurrence and the impact. The idea is to focus on the ones that have a higher probability of occurrence and a significant impact. Those high-priority risks will change over time, and your mitigation plan must change as well. Gupta says, "It's a dynamic process. It's not something you do and then put away for a few years. It's something that you have to keep refreshed."

Smart companies create a feedback process for risk, canvassing external sources to learn about all of the factors that might threaten the ability to create long-term value and disseminating the intelligence throughout the entire company. For instance, WSFS gathers information from all points in the organization where the company gets feedback from its staff and its customers and outsiders—complaints to the call center, the president's office, the Better Business Bureau, and the Consumer Financial Protection Bureau; employee whistleblowers who contact the internal audit and ethics hotline; comments on social media and Gallup nightly customer surveys.

Every month, WSFS captures and sifts through that information to identify specific problems to be addressed and systemic fractures for the company to repair. According to Mark Turner, that regular practice has helped WSFS stay ahead of issues like the one that Wells Fargo inflicted on itself, and its customers, when it opened accounts for people who didn't exist or didn't want them.

Given the swiftly changing nature of risk, boards can't rely on quarterly meetings to ensure that management is properly addressing its mitigation strategy. Staying current between meetings is imperative. Gupta of Delphi says, "You don't want to surprise your board. If some event happens, it is the role of the CEO to alert the board and engage with them in whatever forum they want. That's part of building trust not only with the board but with the shareholders." At Delphi, the CEO would send the board a one- or two-page report, followed by a sixty- or ninety-minute phone call, whenever events arose. Make sure management reports to you on that schedule.

While the strategy and risk committee should play a lead role in the management of risk, the job cannot be left entirely to one body. Accountability must be distributed. The general counsel or a member of a cybersecurity committee can pull together a composite of all risks and make recommendations for addressing them in the future. Then different committees can tackle discrete elements.

Merck learned a dire lesson in the dangers of centralizing risk too tightly. In 2017 it fell victim to NotPetya, the vicious malware that originated in the Ukraine. When its system was infected, NotPetya took Merck down worldwide in the space of eight minutes. The reason it was so vulnerable: its cyber architecture was horizontal and completely connected.

The calamity occurred even though Merck paid quite a lot of attention to the security of its network. Former Ogilvy & Mather CEO Shelly Lazarus, who sits on the Merck board, says the company reviewed cybersecurity on a regular basis. Responsibility for the job rested with the audit committee—not the place we would pick for nonfinancial risk—and the committee periodically brought its reports to the full board. She says, "It was discussed. People were questioned. The CIO would come on a regular basis and talk about everything we were doing for cybersecurity. But no one knew to look at the architecture and say you have this incredible vulnerability because if anyone hacks in, it's all over. There are no walls."

So even though Merck was addressing cybersecurity, clearly it was not seeing the right things. She says, "Cybersecurity risk is with us everywhere. It has to be a constant topic of study and examination. But there's got to be a little bit of humility as well to say that we're not going to see everything and we're not going to find everything." Lazarus spoke with us before the coronavirus pandemic emerged. So count her as prescient when she adds, "We'll never accurately assess where the next risk is coming from. It's going to be something we haven't thought about, and that'll be the one that's really important."

With technology at the heart of every company, whether it is in the technology business or not, overseeing technology risk is an essential task of the board to protect long-term plans. How do smart companies go about it? GM faced challenges on two fronts: cybersecurity of its corporate systems and the safety of its vehicles as they become ever more electronic and connected and, in its Cruise division, self-driving.

One of first moves the board made was to beef up its expertise with a dedicated cybersecurity committee and to bring an aerospace engineer onto the board to head it. Then the company hired a consultant, Booz Allen Hamilton, to do an assessment. GM CEO Mary Barra says, "One of their recommendations was that we needed to pull cyber under one person. We now have one chief cybersecurity information officer," who presides over a dedicated team.

Then GM rolled out the system companywide. It created teams at its Cruise, GM Financial, product development, and traditional IT units. As it examined the issue, complexities emerged. GM has operations around the globe and a tech center in China. Not all of its critical business are completely under its control either, with suppliers and dealers in the mix. So it would need to account for geographic variations and work closely with outsiders to address risk factors in their spheres. The cybersecurity function has its own budget, the same way that audit does. "And if we're making changes to it," says Barra, "we have to go back to the cyber committee of the board."

So the formula here: create an area of responsibility on the board; bring in a consultant to help complete a risk assessment; roll out a risk response companywide, with attention to both business and geographic divisions; obtain cooperation from suppliers and sellers; and create a separate budget for the role as you would for the audit function.

As GM's example shows, risk in big corporations can be extraordinarily complex, both in its breadth and in the challenges of anticipating all eventualities. One way to monitor the complexities is to create a risk dashboard. Former Vanguard CEO Jack Brennan says, "There are operational risks, there's legal risk, there's governmental risk—the agreed-upon risks that are potentially damaging to the value of this company. They should be a topic of discussion at every board meeting. And the Big R risk is reputation risk." Having a risk dashboard would be a good tool to help the board focus quickly.

Some companies try to battle-test their systems. They might offer rewards for employees who are able to hack a system or expose a point of vulnerability. One large company asked the tech staff in an operating division to try to attack a financial unit. Another hired people who had hacked a supplier to run its cybersecurity program. In each case, the company used a prime motivation for behavior that results in technology risk—the satisfaction of cracking a code—and defused it by changing the payout: recognition and a reward.

The Risk of Bad Behavior

Besides external risks and operational vulnerabilities, companies also face risk arising from the behavior of its managers and staff, both malfeasance and poor business practices. The board must develop processes to stay informed about this most dispiriting source of risk. Rogers of T. Rowe Price says, "Oftentimes I worry more about an internal bad actor than I do an external bad actor. Our investments in the area of risk management and risk control seem to increase almost geometrically relative to the amount of time spent on this stuff twenty-five years ago, when it was really kind of an adjunct to an audit committee meeting."

Yet the risk from bad players seems to surprise many companies. For instance, most of what we read about cybersecurity suggests that hacks come principally from North Korea or Russia or China, which we imagine to be pilfering our secrets and publishing our Social Security numbers on the internet. The greater risk might be from your employees.

Smart companies take steps to protect themselves from these bad actors. AbbVie, for example, has systems in place to guard against intellectual property theft by its staff, because if an employee is angry, one way to get back at the employer is to steal data. When staff leave for the day, AbbVie cuts off access to their computer accounts and dumps all their data to a digital location, which it monitors very closely. Perhaps theft is not entirely preventable, but prevention of data loss is a critical need for companies to get their arms around.

The risk of bad behavior is not always a function of venality but of weakness. Warren Buffett of Berkshire Hathaway has observed a myriad of reasons why people diverge from ethical practices. He says, "I would say that it isn't fundamental dishonesty that causes people to go in a different direction. It's human nature. There are plenty of people who are really decent people, intelligent people. I'd be happy if they married my daughter or if they moved in next door to me. But they just don't come to grips with reality. And boards usually don't push them to."

Sometimes performance pressure leads to unsound behavior. The talent, compensation, and execution committee needs to focus on this human element of risk, particularly as it relates to the company's top twenty or thirty people, who carry an outsize influence on operations and can potentially generate considerable harm. For instance, in the mid- to late 1990s, Lucent CEO Rich McGinn attempted to drive revenue growth to very high levels. A full 40 percent of his output went to dot-com companies, and the company leaned heavily on a single supplier. The bubble burst. Lucent's receivables grew considerably and brought the company to its knees. The risk was directly attributable to overweening ambition.

In many ways, bad behavior is a risk associated with a bad corporate culture, which is often associated with the ills at the heart of the wider culture, whether racial discrimination or economic injustice.

Timothy Richmond of AbbVie says, "This risk category is often conceived around audit risk. But look at Boeing. So we've articulated this risk more broadly around human capital. If you've not put a premium on culture and the earning of trust, whether among your community or your own workforce, you've accelerated the risk. And you can't put that back in the bottle."

Richmond believes that the risk of a bad corporate culture has the potential to decimate the company over the long term. Whether people set out to take property or whether they are receiving incentives to engage in poor behavior, damage a company's reputation, or just not care about it, these are cultural elements. Managing them well creates a higher level of expectations in the workforce and ensures that systems and processes are in place to anticipate and forestall problems.

Of the companies whose culture failed—Enron, Tyco, Volkswagen, Wells Fargo—Richmond argues that the root was a failed culture of leadership. He says, "How you accomplish what you do is as important as what you accomplish. How we treat people creates the culture of an enterprise. Otherwise what you say will be misaligned with what you do, and you've created that risk. Culture is not a program. It's a reflection of what you do every day, how you engage, how you react."

For that reason, we recommend that companies adopt a signed code of conduct for all employees detailing the behavioral requirements that undergird cultural expectations. A well-implemented ethical code might have prevented the channel stuffing at Wells Fargo and could have provided a legal basis for firing key staff and managers involved in the offense.

Many companies have codes of conduct, though not all require them to be signed. An example of an excellent and wide-ranging code is Google's. More than six thousand words long, it covers corporate reputation, equal opportunity, bullying, drugs and alcohol, conflicts of interest, customer relations, confidentiality, intellectual property, financial integrity and responsibility, competition and trading law, and government relations, among other subjects. Such codes both help guide employee behavior and protect the company and its customers.

Whether people deviate from ethical behavior through bad intention or bad practices, you must put mechanisms in place to control for divergence from policy or good governance. Buffett often serves on audit committees; companies try to steer him away from the compensation committee, knowing he is famously abstemious in directors' compensation, with Berkshire directors paid an average of $2,700 a year in 2018.

Buffett recalls one company in which Berkshire had a huge investment. He pored over the 10Ks and 10Qs very carefully—a good test of whether someone is a good director—and tried to ask probing questions in meetings. He says, "Finally, after a few years, it was clear to me that the company was just playing games in terms of quarterly numbers. I think they were generally perceived of in the investment community as doing it, but they got cheers for doing it. And I realized that the only way to really get one of the super big-name auditors to behave was to have them more afraid of me than they were afraid of the management."

From then on, he set out four questions for the auditors to answer each year, and he asked them to do it in writing. This is Buffett's test:

1. If the auditor were solely responsible for preparation of the company's financial statements, would they have in any way been prepared differently from the manner selected by management?

2. If the auditor were an investor, would he have received—in plain English—the information essential to his understanding the company's financial performance during the reporting period?

3. Is the company following the same internal audit procedure that would be followed if the auditor himself were CEO? If not, what are the differences and why?

4. Is the auditor aware of any actions—either accounting or operational—that have had the purpose and effect of moving revenues or expenses from one reporting period to another?

These questions only even up the playing field. Much of the required financial reporting material either is designed to obfuscate or has the effect of doing so. Buffett says, "The company lawyers tell you to list every possible thing you can dream of in the 10K just as a protection. And one of those things will have a weight of real potential risk. You had to be totally focused on that, and not twenty other risks. They kill you with quantity. The risk committees almost don't have a chance."

To protect long-term value, demand that your management gives you the information you need to make sure it behaves ethically.

CHECKLIST FOR MANAGING RISK

- Understand the risks associated with each of your critical capabilities.

- Protect your supply chain: have a plan B in case you are cut off from your current suppliers.

- To ensure long-term survival, manage your liquidity, debt, and balance sheet so you have headroom in case of emergencies.

- Avoid the risk of losing crucial talent by creating a budget to retain key employees.

- When planning to merge with another company, demand a human capital audit of your target to ensure you know whether key staff will be staying.

- Make an emergency succession plan for all key workers—not just the CEO and CFO.

- Construct a model for identifying and responding to total enterprise risk—the risks that can upend the entire company.

- Distinguish between risk avoidance and risk management.

- Put systems in place to protect your intellectual property from employee theft.

- Adopt a code of conduct to be signed by all employees.

PART TWO

Best Board Practices

Managing for the New TSR and
Long-Term Value Creation

W hen a company refocuses its attention on talent, strategy, and risk, the old way of doing business won't work for the board any more than it will for managers. The board must have the right people to oversee the new TSR. It must have the right knowledge and the right organization to do its job well. And it must recommit to building its relationships with investors and other stakeholders. The board needs a new playbook, too.

Part two is that playbook. It will give your board members the capabilities and special skills they need to keep the company on track at a time of great change. It will help you structure committees so that the directors have the time to apply their expertise and delve into issues

The new value playbook

Upgrade **CAPABILITIES**	**Normalize board** turnover **Choose** the right leader **Optimize** executive sessions	**Redefine** mandates **Create** new committees **Conserve** the board's time	*Redesign* **COMMITTEES**
Diversify **INFORMATION**	**Recruit** diverse viewpoints **Consider** all data sources **Analyze** your competitors	**Anticipate** investors' concerns **Communicate** regularly **Upgrade** investor relations	*Engage* **INVESTORS**

crucial to governance. It will point the way to the resources you must tap so that the board has an independent source of information. And it will show you how to deal with investors, both to learn from them and to protect your company.

With this playbook in hand, the board can make managing for the long term its true focus.

UPGRADE
CAPABILITIES

CHAPTER 4

Creating a Capable Board

Managing for talent, strategy, and risk starts with managing the talent of the board. Just as for the managerial ranks, a board needs the right human capital to meet its goals for creating long-term value. It must have the right composition to manage talent, strategy, and risk. It must have the right leadership to achieve consensus on its plans. And it must have systems in place to change and refresh its membership as the needs of the company evolve.

The board must also overcome impediments to its work, including lack of time, lack of expertise, lack of diversity, and lack of knowledge about markets, competitors, and the new digital economy. And the board should be benchmarked not only against its peer group of publicly traded companies but also against private equity.

In this chapter, we'll give the board a new guide for managing its own talent. The mandate for the new TSR will redefine the board's composition. The board must have not only members versed in today's business but also those who will be right for tomorrow's strategy. And with companies in all industries retooling for the digital age, the new playbook demands the presence of directors who are able to make that leap.

We look at board capability in two ways: through the intrinsic abilities of the directors and through the processes the board has in place to exercise its power. Yet in discussions of board capability and composition, the word "leadership" is absent in almost every part of the literature.

Most boards don't have a robust system to ensure that the directors are doing their job, either. Indeed, many directors view board evaluations as a joke and do not take them seriously. Rarely are board members fired or pulled aside and told they aren't measuring up. For a lot of directors, once they are on the board, they are on it for good, like an appointment to the Supreme Court. As a result, many CEOs say that one or two directors on their board could vanish overnight and they wouldn't even miss them. That must change.

Good boards are taking steps to enhance their effectiveness. They are doing more to develop the expertise they need to fully understand the work of the company. And they are adopting measures to hold their own members accountable. The goal is that over time, the board will develop independence of mind and construct a framework to understand the outside world of customers, competitors, and markets against which it makes decisions. A board's willingness to change how it functions will determine whether it builds value or destroys it. With these methods, we will help you create it. (See figure 4-1.)

A Board with the Skills for Tomorrow

To do a good job of managing talent, strategy, and risk for the long term, the board must assemble its members with the care of any elite team. The essential attributes of an effective board: it must have the right mix of capabilities and competencies, with members who

FIGURE 4-1

The new value playbook: Capabilities

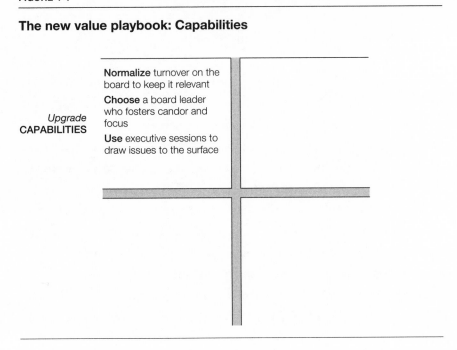

Upgrade
CAPABILITIES

Normalize turnover on the board to keep it relevant

Choose a board leader who fosters candor and focus

Use executive sessions to draw issues to the surface

can chair audit committees and understand digital technology; it must be flexible enough to adapt quickly when conditions change; and it should satisfy objectives for diversity of experience, age, and gender.

The board should have rigorous criteria for selection, especially for leadership roles. But you can start with a simple exercise: write down what you think you need in a director—today and in the future—and why you need it, whether it is to make the transition to a new business, or to build the business aggressively, or to be sustainable in the long term. And decide whether any of those changes require a cultural shift in the board.

From there, smart companies are taking steps to rebuild the know-how that their boards have lost over time, especially compared with management. (For more on the asymmetry of information between the board and management, see chapter 6.) The boards of fifty or sixty years ago did not have a lot of independence, but because their membership included many retired executives, the directors knew a lot about the subject matter.

Then boards changed. As State Street's Ron O'Hanley says, "We went to trophy boards where you lost the industry expertise." The directors may have been luminaries in their fields, but they didn't know the business of the companies they were meant to oversee. Now the pendulum is swinging back, and companies are putting together boards with both industry know-how and the functional expertise necessary now and for the future. Boards are becoming more diverse and inclusive as well, though too often that goal is still aspirational.

So the mandate for boards is to strike the right balance between industry insiders and outsiders. If you overstock the board with industry experts, you risk having a board that will overrun management. A board that draws all its members from the same industry will be bounded by that unitary experience and prone to groupthink and myopia. Real and effective exchange with the world beyond the company requires wider representation. Rapid change is transforming industries across the economy. To navigate those currents, you need people on the board from other businesses.

With long-term value in mind, smart boards are adding directors with expertise in industries that will be crucial to the work of the company in the years ahead. Coca-Cola's board is a who's who of policy makers and former CEOs, including Herb Allen and Barry Diller. In 2018, it added Caroline Tsay, the CEO of cloud computing company Compute Software and former vice president of software at Hewlett Packard Enterprise. Her background in twenty-first-century technology will help the company move forward with social media initiatives and millennial consumers. Directors like her are comfortable asking uncomfortable questions about her area of experience and are also willing to ask the dumb question about the company's business.

Every boardroom should have digital expertise. Indeed, the leading area of board search in corporate America today may be cybersecurity. Former T. Rowe Price chair Brian Rogers says, "If you've had a good career at the NSA down the road here in Maryland, you can probably become a director of three companies very quickly. You don't want to rely solely on your internal IT people for this role, and, at the same time, it's a hard slot to fill."

Be ready to cast a wide net: essential technological expertise can come from far afield. People who think differently about disruption, and particularly disruption by technology, can come from any industry. That's because the agenda for technology has changed. For a long time, technology was about what a business needed to run well and to innovate, and only then about the customer. Now it's the reverse. Today, technology is what the customer wants. The board's job is to bring the customer experience into the company's own systems to create the products of the future.

Boards should also have at least one member from private industry versed in the specifics of moneymaking models—financial engineering, fundraising, and the use of experts to improve long-term cost productivity, margins, cash flow, and capital structure. Executives from private equity have experience using such measures to buy companies and then develop a more innovative business model, creating greater value for the long term. They are adept at finding different ways to price products and increase sales. They know the fundamentals of moneymaking because their lives depend on it. So we love the idea of recruiting someone who brings those skills to the board and who can teach the other directors new ways to create revenues and generate data about company performance.

Ensuring that you have the right skills on the board for the long term is a continuous process. Michele Hooper of the Directors' Council says, "To me, the skills matrix is a living document. When I chaired the nomination and governance committee, we talked about it at least once a quarter. It's not something you trot out once a year. It's something that you're constantly looking at." Seek outside perspective to help identify needs. The board of UnitedHealth Group, on which Hooper sits, shares its skills matrix with an advisory committee. She says, "We ask them for their input. Are these the right skills and experiences that will help us long term? Do you think we need to tweak it?"

As you consider your board membership, keep in mind that size matters. Overly large boards are counterproductive. Having too many people in the room can hamper free debate and discussion. We think the optimal size for a board is ten directors—nine from outside the company and one from inside, or sometimes eight and two.

Not every skill you want in the boardroom has to be resident on the board. You can have success by bringing in experts to help you think through any aspect of your business, whether a new technology or a competitive threat. But you will have to weigh and prioritize what you need in the boardroom to make your decision. What skills do you have at the table, and what skills can you bring to the table? If the specialists you need don't live in your boardroom, invite them in for a visit. The flexibility will help you create long-term value as you adjust to doing business in a world where needs might change radically in an instant.

Beyond looking for directors with the right skills and experience, boards need to do more to increase the diversity of their membership. To meet this goal, be prepared to go off the beaten track. For its two most recent board appointments, Estée Lauder chose people in their thirties to gain expertise in social media, technology, and millennial relations. The company had also been looking to appoint a woman of color. Lady Lynn Forester de Rothschild, head of the nominating and board affairs committee there, says, "We didn't hire a search firm because we knew that the names we were looking for would not be on their list." Instead they solicited names from Wei Christianson, a board member who runs Morgan Stanley in Asia, and Mellody Hobson, a Black business leader.

Lady Lynn, who is also cofounder of the hedge fund Inclusive Capital Partners, began interviewing a slate of twenty with executive director William Lauder. She says, "I had the most exciting week of my life in Silicon Valley and San Francisco interviewing these women. We ended up with two women when we were only looking for one. I definitely think a concerted effort to find women and people who aren't the usual suspects brings an enormous amount to a board."

Too often, though, diversity initiatives are box-ticking exercises. When the choice for a board candidate is a toss-up between a man and a woman, Warren Buffett prefers to vote for the woman because in the past, women often lost out just because they were female. Yet many of the efforts to redress these circumstances are cosmetic.

So he tries to approach recruitment with a greater sense of purpose. Buffett says,

> Headhunters frequently call me and say, "We're looking for a female director." I have yet to hear one of them say, "We're looking for a female director who is owner-oriented and business-savvy." They're looking for somebody who has a name that will reflect well on the company. I do think that women have gotten a raw deal for so long that I'd absolutely prefer to give the job to a female. But I've never recommended a woman who I didn't think had the qualities that I've set forth in the ten-year report.

In other words, make diversity real, not a pretense.

The Essence of a Great Director

More than any set of abilities you might find on a résumé, the ability to be a good director is a personality trait. It involves qualities of insight, outlook, and character. Yes, boards that have deep industry knowledge tend to be more strategic and focus more on the long term. But strategy is a way of thinking, relying on judgment and experience. The directors who come in to reshape a business are often from outside the industry. Transformation is their skill.

Your prerequisite in selecting board members should be breadth of vision and leadership ability; only then should you consider whether a candidate has the background and expertise you want. These attributes have nothing to do with age. Some people at twenty-five have a broader perspective and are more powerful leaders than far older peers.

Great board members have an almost paradoxical ability to be collegial and constructive on the one hand and challenging on the other. Brendan Swords, CEO of Wellington Management, says, "You want humility and courage. The best board members have good listening skills. They've got thick skin. They're willing to speak without fear and ask hard questions. They're fully prepared. They're highly engaged. They're open-minded." By contrast, the worst board members have poor listening skills. He says, "They're like bulls in a china shop and are always pushing their own thesis, their own agenda, to the exclusion of all others."

You can tell good board members from bad ones by the questions they ask. In any boardroom, it's easy to distinguish the directors who really try to get inside the company, traveling to different regions and spending time with local staff, from those who just show up at the meetings. For that reason, seek board members who are ready to work hard. Having board members with the time and energy to invest will help eliminate management's information advantage. To that end, be sure that you know what motivated the director to join the board. Otherwise you may find that their contribution doesn't live up to their résumé.

Look for board members who have the courage of their convictions. We hope that Boeing has board members who can resist short-term pressures and instead think about long-term issues, and about how to do the right thing for all constituents, not just the shareholders. In thinking of the company's travails, Mary Erdoes of J.P. Morgan Asset & Wealth Management says, "If you ask what a good board member is, it's someone who refuses to be handled and knows when they're being handled, because it's very easy for a company to do."

So, beware of management attempts to stock the board with pawns. In his letter to shareholders in the 2019 Berkshire Hathaway annual report, Buffett writes that the CEO of a company searching for board members will almost certainly check with a candidate's current CEO about whether this person is a "good" director—"good" being a code word meant to avoid pollution by anyone who has challenged the present CEO's compensation or acquisition schemes. As Buffett puts it, "When seeking directors, CEOs don't look for pit bulls. It's the cocker spaniel that gets taken home."

A genuinely good board member can combine the best traits of a CEO and an investor. Buffett brings both attributes to the boards on which he sits. He says, "I come at boards with a little different perspective in that I operate as an executive with a board. I've been in small companies and large companies, and I have seen how boards are a combination of a legal organization and a social organization. How they perform depends, to some extent, on the objectives and personality of the CEO."

That's why we like to see two people with CEO experience on every board. Only a CEO knows what the CEO's job is—an essential insight when selecting a new leader for the company. Often a CEO search led by a non-CEO feels like it's in the hands of amateurs. You also want to have CEOs in the boardroom when things go south. They are most likely to make the tough calls and least likely to run for the exits.

But don't assume that someone will be a good director just because they have a good record as a CEO at another company. Some former CEOs hated what they deemed to be meddlesome behavior by their own boards and may make corresponding accommodations to the CEO somewhere else. Ed Garden of Trian Partners says, "It's amazing how respected CEOs who have impressive résumés and who generated impressive shareholder return add no value in the boardroom of their new company. It depends on their willingness to learn about the business, to challenge the CEO and the social dynamic in the boardroom, and to be provocative and facilitate debate." For that reason, he would be leery of appointing a sitting CEO to the board: "They are simply too busy running their own company."

In any case, avoid putting the outgoing CEO of your own company on the board. The presence of the former boss can crimp the style of the new incumbent and complicate matters for the board in its dealings with management. A crucial element in discussions with management is confrontation with reality. Elena Botelho at ghSMART says, "How many boards do you know where there's really honest dialogue? Where people say, 'All right, this acquisition didn't go well. So now let's make the most out of it. How do we learn from it?'" The uncomfortable questions frequently come from smart, competent people who aren't former CEOs—the scientist or the technologist who is willing to probe and who doesn't assume that everything is going to be OK. The presence of the old CEO can inhibit such discussions, with the other directors reluctant to criticize decisions made by their peer.

The Right Leadership

However capable the individual directors are, for the board to do its job well, it must have a leader who can focus debate on the issues that matter and arrive at a consensus. The problem is that many boards devote far less attention and formal discussion to future board leadership than they do to the skills and experience necessary for future directors and committee heads. Korn Ferry vice chair Joseph Griesedieck says, "We find this to be an anomaly in board planning, particularly given the impact that an effective independent board chairman or lead director can have in shaping the overall culture of the board and encouraging the directors to behave in ways that increase the board's effectiveness."

Having a powerful lead independent director (LID) is essential, especially if your CEO is also the chair. There's nothing wrong with combining those two roles; doing so can be beneficial in difficult times. If you're speaking to the press or testifying before Congress, having a single voice becomes quite powerful.

But even if the roles of CEO and chair are separate, you still need an additional strong leader. A good LID will serve as a counterbalance to the CEO and hold the CEO accountable. The lead director must be truly independent. Abe Friedman, founder of CamberView Partners and former BlackRock managing director, says, "Often the person who gets selected to be LID is a buddy of the CEO." That state of affairs complicates matters for another board member who wants to raise an issue. The independent director structure allows for openness.

In choosing a lead director, think first of the skills and experience that would make this person effective. The best candidate may not be the one who has served on the board the longest or who has the most industry knowledge. It's the one who is able to rationalize disparate points of view and bring them to the table.

The Right Setting

However strong its leadership, for the board to work effectively, the directors will need a setting that allows them to share information among themselves without pressure from management. In the early 1990s, some of the directors in a handful of companies began to meet in private. Many of these directors belonged to clubs and met there. And in some instances, a CEO from one company who was sitting on the board of another began to raise questions about performance there. At American Express, Jim Robinson III was riding high, known in some circles as corporate America's secretary of state because of the relationships he built around the world. But his reconception of the company as a unified financial store, built through acquisitions, was foundering. The directors, in their private huddle, agreed on a course of action: they would remove Robinson from the job. But the process was entirely sub rosa.

As an alternative to secretiveness, the idea arose to institutionalize meetings of directors with the knowledge of the CEO and develop a methodology to evaluate the CEO and air concerns. The aim was to make the mechanisms transparent so directors didn't have to act as a cabal. Any independent director would be able to raise any issue to see if a consensus existed on the board and determine a course of action, such as a further investigation. In due time, after soliciting the input of the entire board, the independent directors—led by the nonexecutive chair or the lead director—would feed back suggestions to the CEO or the management team. These meetings would become the executive session.

They are now a pillar for how the board can meet without the pressure of management—essential for effective oversight of talent, strategy, and risk. Warren Buffett says, "I've probably been a little more of a skunk at the garden party than most directors when I'm on a board, but I've been inhibited in a significant way from raising questions. The lead director was a huge improvement because the average person recoils from starting to hold rump meetings. So here was finally a vehicle that let directors meet in a nonsecretive, approved, socially acceptable, comfortable manner where they could discuss things that they didn't discuss when the CEO was in the room."

Different companies have different practices for executive sessions. For many, the CEO will attend the first part of the session so that the independent directors can get the information they want and hear whatever issues the CEO wishes to raise. The independent directors will then excuse the CEO, and an open session among them will follow.

The skill of the chair in the executive session is crucial. The idea is to pinpoint issues worthy of debate—one or two or three per meeting at most—rather than producing a laundry list of concerns, some inevitably unimportant. In many companies, the lead director will talk to the independent directors one-on-one every quarter to plan the agenda for the following meeting, ensuring continuity.

Boards frequently hold their executive sessions after each board meeting. This practice creates problems. The directors are likely to start peeking at their watches to see when they'll be able to leave. And directors may spend the session reviewing and critiquing the presentations raised earlier in the day, thus focusing on short-term concerns and operational minutia instead of issues related to long-term value.

A better way is to have the executive session first thing in the morning, before the board meeting begins. The CEO can then set the mood for the session and focus the group on what is to come later in the day. After the CEO leaves, the independent directors can decide if they wish to raise other matters. They then have a chance to reflect before the board meeting. The result is a forward-thinking session, followed by an opportunity to react to the CEO's presentation.

Having open, well-conducted executive sessions can help short-circuit the difficult feelings that can arise through the workings of informal networks. These networks can be quite efficient in delivering worrisome information to the CEO. Every CEO has one or two friends on the board who will report what was said in meetings and who said it; indeed, the CEO would be foolish not to have such allies. Existence of these subterranean lines of communication can impede discussion in the boardroom. Gradually, open executive sessions can create an atmosphere of transparency, candor, and honesty. Over time, when word gets back of frank discussions in the boardroom, the CEO will see them as constructive.

In executive sessions, it's important to focus on the right things. Some directors like the idea of former CEOs asking sharp questions of management, but these contributions must deal with issues that matter and not be designed merely to show that the CEO is still in the know. A renowned CEO on a board with which one of us is associated said, "I think the cost of capital is 8 percent, not 7 percent." Contributions like that one can spoil a meeting because they are so trivial. To move the dialogue forward, ask the right questions and home in on the big issues. In full board sessions, strive for continuity and cogency. As we'll show you in chapter 5, committees are the best place for detail work, fine-tuning, and mastering a subject.

Assessing the Board

Since the board is a company's governing authority, responsibility for its evaluation falls to the board itself. The only way for the process to work is to institutionalize it through adoption of a charter with guidelines to assess performance.

Done well, self-evaluation can be a good device to help directors change their behavior or to make a different kind of contribution to

board initiatives. But the job is rarely done well. At too many companies, appointment to the board is for all practical purposes permanent.
As a consequence, some boards are littered with ineffective members,
without a mechanism for clearing them out. So the board must strive
to identify good ways of refreshing its membership and making its activities more effective.

The goal of self-evaluation is not the sort of performance review that
one might conduct for a manager or employee. The board is a different
institution with a different purpose. Who would evaluate Warren Buffett's performance on the board of Coca-Cola, on which he served for
seventeen years? Rather, the process should involve constructive, specific feedback from peers about what a director could consider doing
more of, or less of, or differently. Feedback can come from management as well as board members. The idea is to learn whether the board
has added value and where, if it has failed and why, and what it needs
to do going forward.

The tools and techniques of board self-evaluation have evolved over
the years, but not far enough. One method that became common in the
past was a checklist of twenty or thirty questions, much like the ones
that have been common for CEOs (see chapter 1). For instance: Does
the board member come to all meetings? Are they prepared? Are they
on time? These are hygiene questions. They don't tell you very much.
As a result, boards typically haven't done very much in response.

For lead directors, the practice is even worse. In the early 2010s, one
of us (Carey) convened a group of thirty-three lead directors and non-
executive chairs and asked if the board evaluates anyone in the room
on the quality of their performance. Not one hand went up. So while
corporations have established the concept of the lead director, almost
no one subjects this person to evaluation.

At best, many boards just check the box on board evaluations. Very
few fire the nonproductive director. They look the other way and give
the director a pass, letting them run out their term for another two or
three years if the board isn't elected annually. That sort of favor can put

the company in a bind if other directors look for the same treatment. The outcome could be a continual impediment to refreshing the board.

We need a different process, both for individual directors and for the board as a whole. For the most trenchant evaluations, interviews are far superior to checklists. The questions can be more pointed, and directors will have a chance to prepare. Twenty or thirty minutes per interview should be sufficient.

Any of four parties can oversee the process of interviewing directors, collecting data, and preparing a report: the lead director or non-executive chair, the general counsel of the company, a legal firm, or a consultant. Bill McCracken of CA Technologies likes to use outside groups to assist in evaluations because the egalitarian nature of boards can make judging fellow members difficult. He says, "Boards are peer groups. They're not hierarchical. Even when you look at the board chairs, it's a leader leading leaders."

Feedback to individual directors and the board as a whole should always come from two people—the CEO and either the lead director or the chair. Having two people leading the feedback sessions prevents miscommunication. The lead director working alone might not elicit a candid view; by contrast, someone from outside the boardroom can push the director to be more specific. The CEO can give pointed insights to each member of the board and to the board as a whole. Avoid using paper; it is discoverable, and people don't like it.

CEOs can help directors perform better by setting clear goals. Elena Botelho of ghSMART says, "The most powerful, impressive individuals do best when they know what contribution is expected of them." These effective CEOs avoid micromanaging, which helps the other board members be vocal in the boardroom. One of the CEOs Botelho works with was about to lose a valuable board member. She learned that this director had no clear mandate. She asked the CEO, "In your dream world, where would you have this person contribute?"

The director was an expert in M&A, and the company happened to be ramping up its acquisition strategy. Botelho and the CEO asked the director for help with this initiative, and the board member decided to stay. Botelho says, "The board member went from feeling they're just having a set of good conversations to feeling they can really have an impact."

In assessing the lead director, the focus of the evaluation should be on the past and future performance of the board as a whole. We recommend selecting a group of three directors to establish the three or four major roles or responsibilities that will fall to the board for the coming year, as well as plans by the board to create value for the long term.

Boards can make measurable ad hoc contributions, too. For instance, when PepsiCo management proposed several acquisitions that would have been contrary to the company's low-sugar strategy, the board voted it down. And as we saw in chapter 3, when Catalent's CEO hesitated to make what would prove to be a transformational acquisition because of the cost, the board said to proceed and pay the price. These contributions to value are not what you would think of as an activity, but they stand out. Boards don't make such contributions every day, or every year; they may take two or three years to emerge. These can be part of the lead director's evaluation as well.

At the end of the year, the group of three will assess the lead director based on how well the board performed its tasks. If the group decides that the lead director was ineffective, the board can offer coaching to improve performance depending on the faults—perhaps inattention during meetings, or taking the side of certain board members against others. Or it can remove the lead director from the job.

For the evaluation process to be useful, candor is essential. Boards might believe they have great directors who have served them well. But do they have the right talent in place? They may or may not. Michele Hooper of the Directors' Council says, "We have to become more honest with ourselves about who is sitting around the table. Some people would use the word 'ruthless.' Unfortunately, we don't have enough time to retool and retrain our more experienced board members for the twenty-first century."

Refreshing the Board

Board tenures should thus not only allow members to develop proficiency but also ensure regular turnover so that the mix on the board can change with conditions in the outside world. Anne Mulcahy, former CEO of Xerox, recommends seven-year terms for directors, renewable up to two times. The defined tenure will dissuade directors from holding on longer than they might wish to. Some directors could be ready to leave but fear that if they resign, people will think something is wrong with their performance, so they hang on to keep their reputation intact. A term limit gives them an out.

Refreshing the board is more important than retaining continuity of experience. Jack Brennan, formerly of Vanguard, agrees that term limits should be a core part of board structure to force refreshment without making it personal. He says, "The challenge is that the company faces change, people's skills decay, their experiences become less relevant. People say, 'You lose institutional memory.' I think it's a small price to pay for what you get from board refreshment." He recommends a ten-person board with two or three seats that rotate every two or three years.

But we would counsel against a mandatory retirement age. It's a blunt instrument. Half the board members may be people you would love to keep; the other half you may wish had left five years earlier. Some companies will automatically drop the bottom 10 percent of the directors based on a rating. That method is arbitrary and unfair. Don't substitute rules for judgment.

Boards can retool their refreshment processes to make life easier for both those who remain and those who leave. Nobody likes to embarrass a fellow director, and nobody likes to be fired, no matter how you sugarcoat the news. Only if you master the process can you keep the board evergreen.

Some companies use a directors' review as a cover to trigger refreshment. Ivan Seidenberg, former Verizon CEO, would ask each board member which of the present directors they would select if the company was going to keep just seven. He found that the lists from all the directors were almost identical. In the review that followed, he could then tell each director about the result of the poll and present it as the choice of the peer group. For the ones not on the favorites list, he would suggest that they consider retiring in two years. That process avoids embarrassment; no one becomes the enemy, because the recommendation is a democratic vote. As such, it is highly subjective, but the crowdsourcing spreads the responsibility.

Attributing changes to a consultant's review can ease the way to refreshment as well. A consultant might survey all the members of the board about the performance of the other directors, asking at the end of an interview for a simple pass-fail rating. Any director who fails two years in a row will be off the board. Make the decision clinical and definitive, and not up for discussion. Implementing any other sort of performance management system is difficult because directors want to be nice to one another. It may be that nobody will say anything bad because they don't want a colleague to be fired. But then the fault is collectively the board's.

For new directors, be ready to act quickly if performance is not up to par. Our recommendation: a director should be proficient within four board meetings. (The exception is the audit committee, which does the heavy lifting on risk oversight, and whose head must be proficient from day one.) If the director isn't performing well, offer coaching. If you see no sign of improvement after another six months, begin the process of asking the director to leave. The position matters too much for the long-term growth of the company to waste any time.

Replacing a board member without alarming the others takes delicacy. Asking a board member to leave because they are not contributing or because the company's needs have changed is hard, but not the most difficult part of removing a director. Raj Gupta of Delphi Automotive says, "The important issue is not the board member you're asking to leave. He or she is gone. It's how the others perceive this, so that they don't start looking over their shoulder and watching their behavior and being careful. That's not what you want." Rather than asking directors to step out right away, Gupta advises giving them time to leave so that no one feels they've been pushed.

You can lay the groundwork for turnover by creating expectations. Several years ago, GM's Mary Barra decided that even though they were superior people, two board members did not have the skills and background GM would need in the years ahead. She says, "With respect but with transparency, we talked with them about where the company was going. If they're not the right person for the job, it doesn't mean they're a bad person, whether it's a board member or a senior leader of the company. If you can lay a foundation that way, it makes a difficult conversation slightly less difficult." In 2015, to meet its coming needs for technical expertise, GM appointed Linda Gooden, former executive vice president of Lockheed Martin, to the board for her strong engineering background. She now chairs the cybersecurity committee.

The key advantage of the approach taken by Verizon, Vanguard, Delphi, and GM compared with immediate removal is that the two-year window allows time to plan. The directors who will be leaving can drop hints to their friends elsewhere that they will be looking to move to another board. And the board's nomination and governance committee will have time to fill the coming vacancies and can act now to identify candidates based on intelligence about changing markets, technology, and competition. Both the self-evaluation process and input from management about the long-term course of the business will be crucial in deciding which skills to seek in new directors.

Compensation: How to Pay the Board

The chief goal of a board compensation policy is to ensure long-term alignment of the interests of the directors and those of the shareholders. Back in the days when board compensation was mostly in cash, directors faced very little pressure to represent the shareholders. Now, most big companies award compensation as a fifty-fifty mix of cash and preferred stock, with a variety of vesting periods.

Flexibility is the rule; one size doesn't fit all. But the best model will require directors to invest for three to five years, with an option to take compensation wholly in stock. We favor awarding directors more stock than cash and requiring board members to invest their own money in the company. This approach will give directors a personal incentive to drive long-term shareholder value. And it will reinforce the goal of creating growth through a focus on talent, strategy, and risk.

There are many variations on this theme, all with the goal of creating a stronger alignment between the board's equity compensation and the shareholders. One option is that on joining the board, a director will receive an up-front ten-year stock grant with a vesting every year. Instead of an annual payment of $150,000, the director would get $1.5 million at the outset and would have a strong incentive to make that investment grow. Also consider granting stock awards that the director cannot sell for a number of years after leaving the board. Both measures will keep the directors thinking long term—a model of how the new boardroom playbook can reinforce the goals of the new TSR.

Besides doing little to encourage alignment with shareholders, excessive cash compensation can skew the behavior of board members and attract the wrong sort of director. In his 2019 letter to shareholders, Warren Buffett writes, "Director compensation has now soared to a level that inevitably makes pay a subconscious factor affecting the behavior of many nonwealthy members. Think, for a moment, of the director earning $250,000 to $300,000 for board meetings consuming a pleasant couple of days six or so times a year. Frequently, the possession of one such directorship bestows on its holder three to four times the annual median income of U.S. households."

Directors should be willing to invest in the stock. When their own money is at risk, the imperative to drive long-term appreciation will be even stronger. A number of *Fortune* 500 companies encourage such investment, but don't demand it. Instead they require directors to own stock at some multiple of their annual compensation within a certain number of years, often five. Directors don't have to lay out the money up front; they can reach the goal by electing to receive all of their compensation in stock. That model allows for diversity of age, experience, and income by opening board membership to people without a lot of wealth.

Incentives matter as much as risk. When directors take compensation in stock or buy stock with their own money, they do more than take on risk. They also gain a chance of a greater reward than cash compensation would give them, encouraging long-term thinking.

Consider a board member who receives compensation of $400,000 and elects to take it all in stock, which the director can keep for ten years. If the stock price moves, the accumulated gain is a very large number, on which the director pays capital gains. If the director took compensation in cash, short-term taxes would be due each year; assuming the director invested the rest in equivalents, the long-term return would be far lower. And if the investment spurs the director to look for ideas to improve the company's competitiveness, the return will grow even more.

This mindset creates a multiplier effect of its own. When they are recruiting new people for the board, directors will seek candidates who are likely to have value-creating ideas for managing talent, strategy, and risk—ideas that can increase the multiple of their own investment. If good management is about the creation of virtuous circles, this sort of compensation scheme should be a part of it.

CHECKLIST FOR CREATING A CAPABLE BOARD

- Avoid appointing too many industry insiders to the board to prevent myopia and groupthink.

- Cast a wide net for digital expertise on your board to capture change in adjacent industries.

- Recruit at least one board member from private equity who is versed in the value-creating methods of moneymaking models.

- Look for breadth of vision in board leadership candidates; then consider skills.

- Beware of management attempts to stock the board with pawns.

- Seek at least two board members with CEO experience to make sure you have directors who know the pressures of the job.

- Ensure you have a powerful lead independent director to focus debate and marshal action.

- Use pointed interviews, instead of questionnaires, to evaluate directors.

- Evaluate the lead director according to the performance of the entire board.

- Require directors to invest in the company, either directly or through the compensation they receive for their service.

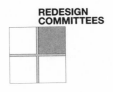

CHAPTER 5

Redesigning the Board's Committees

In meeting its responsibilities, the board has a singular constraint: time. A typical board might meet for only fifty hours a year—nowhere near enough time to develop the depth of knowledge necessary to oversee talent, strategy, and risk. As part of its new playbook, the board should elevate the work of its committees so that the directors can dig deep and manage their agenda.

This way of working is closer to how privately held companies function as they help the CEO create long-term value. Indeed, redesigning the committees for the new TSR will transform the way in which the board and the CEO collaborate. It's through the committees that the board can best establish its working relationship with the CEO.

Committees can facilitate quality, depth, and informality of conversation. Their size and focus can help directors explore ideas with the CEO and build relationships and trust. They allow for a candid give-and-take and let directors and management express different points of view without hurting anyone's feelings. That dynamic will help the CEO succeed.

The committee structure can also help stakeholders from outside the company understand the board's work. Ron O'Hanley of State Street says, "The first thing we look at is how the board goes about effectively overseeing the talent acquisition and development process, the strategy process, and the risk process. How does the board intervene? For strategy in particular, boards don't get to spend enough time. We've made boards so busy for lots of different reasons that strategy always gets pushed to the end of the meeting or to the annual board strategy offsite." A division of labor will redress this problem.

We propose that the board revamp itself around two new committees: the talent, compensation, and execution committee, which will oversee recruitment and pay of senior management and monitor their performance; and the strategy and risk committee, which will have prime responsibility for eliminating the board's asymmetry of information with management. Each of these committees should have four or five members; three of them should be independent directors. The two committees should also have cross-membership, with one director in common.

To manage for the new TSR, the directors need knowledge. They also need the time to think and reflect. And to give them that time, the board must use its committees well, with each able to delve into the issues related to their special briefs. (See figure 5-1.)

Organizing the Committees

For committees to be effective, their work must be clearly defined. The responsibilities and lines of communication of some committees already have that clarity. The role of the audit committee is largely structured by laws and regulations. And since the audit committee

FIGURE 5-1

The new value playbook: Committees

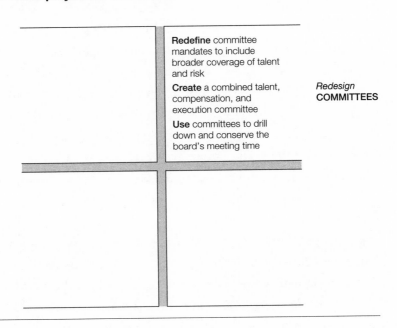

Redefine committee mandates to include broader coverage of talent and risk

Create a combined talent, compensation, and execution committee

Use committees to drill down and conserve the board's meeting time

Redesign
COMMITTEES

must link with internal and external auditors, the way they work together is fairly well established.

For other committees, the board must do more to clarify the depth and focus of their work. Most important, to be effective collaborators with management, the committees must take care to be independent of it. To meet those goals, the chair of each committee must take a strong leadership position. Today, committee chairs rarely seek to develop their own sources of analysis, expertise, or even judgment. That must change.

Besides giving board members the time and wherewithal they need to do their jobs, the committee structure can help the lead director become more effective and knowledgeable. In 2019, one of us (Carey) identified seven *Fortune* 500 companies, including Phillips 66, in which the lead director serves ex officio on all committees, sitting in on meetings on an impromptu basis. Doing so gives the lead director or nonexecutive chair insight into the deliberations of the committees before they present to the full board. We also recommend having either the lead director or one of the other committee chairs, selected on a rotating basis, sit in on every committee meeting, which will help facilitate the selection and appraisal of committee heads.

The lead director should have the responsibility for appointing the committee chairs and should assess their performance annually as well. The lead director should also create a succession plan for the chairs and should move directors through a variety of committees to give them perspective on the entire company. Because of their greater responsibility and the demands on their time, we recommend paying the committee chairs a higher fee than the other directors—perhaps $75,000 more per year.

As part of its brief, each committee should assess management and share its conclusions with the whole board in executive session—focusing on where management can do better and where the board can offer coaching. In turn, the CEO and the management team should evaluate each of the committees to help determine which ones add value and which do not.

The committees should have a clear twelve-month plan for their work and their goals, and they must keep the board up to date on their agenda at meetings throughout the year. That communication is essential to ensure that the board is fully informed when making critical choices, such as CEO selection, merger and acquisition decisions, capital structure plans, allocation of resources for future growth, and trade-offs between short-term and long-term objectives—all at the heart of managing for the new TSR.

Talent, Compensation, and Execution Committee

This committee will oversee key functions that most companies address separately but that ought to be coordinated.

Talent

The most important role of the committee is to understand the changing mix of capabilities that the company will need for the long term and the pathways for improving talent as conditions change. An example of where this function is crucial might be a company whose specialty is mechanical engineering but that must shift its focus to software engineering.

The committee should also prepare for CEO succession. It must identify and learn as much as it can about second- and third-generation CEO candidates and their development paths. Looking further ahead, the committee should identify CEO candidates in different age ranges as well as candidates for other essential senior posts—the CFO and the CHRO primary among them. Candidates for those roles should be geared for future needs.

Besides making sure it is familiar with the quality and strength of the company's management team, the committee should also continually map out who is available elsewhere. For instance, it should know the top three CFOs in its industry in case its own should leave, and it should track them, like football players. Indeed, it should apply the recruiting principles of sports teams to its executive team.

Compensation

Compensation and the basis on which it is determined drive the behavior, focus, and concentration of almost every human being. In companies, compensation is the lever that can determine the behavior of the top fifteen or twenty executives as they exercise their judgment on the balance between short-term and long-term objectives.

Having a compensation committee is also a legal requirement. One of its central roles is to set out the principles that guide compensation policy. To do so, directors must delve deeply into the company's business and its competitive marketplace. They should base their policy not on past performance but on the innovations relevant to performance now and in the future.

Public companies must do more to close the gap with private equity in how they compensate key employees. All compensation committees at public companies use outside consultants. Private equity companies do, too, but they also have tools that more effectively reward exceptional performance. A private equity firm might grant extraordinary shares or options to executives for a certain level of achievement, and if someone is failing, it will withhold money or even fire the person.

The committee can help the board maintain control over company compensation. Once the committee knows the talent in the company, the CEO won't easily be able to deviate from the committee's assessments. By developing knowledge and a database about talent both inside the company and among its competitors, the committee will build the expertise necessary to represent shareholders.

Execution

A key role of this committee will be to monitor performance over time so that it can understand the causes of failure and success in each of the company's lines of business. It will have the power to get external data on the competition and the marketplace and compare the company's performance with that of its peers. And it will decide what the performance measures will be.

The committee should undertake this analysis transparently and with the knowledge of the CEO. The work should be collaborative. The goal is to help the CEO and to detect unacceptable behavior by management, such as units that pull results forward from future periods to meet quarterly estimates or that cut ads just to hold down current expenditures. In other words, the committee will help the CEO perform a culture audit.

The committee should also give backbone to the CEO and absorb pressure from shareholders when the company doesn't make its quarterly numbers, keeping the right balance between short-term and long-term goals. A committee can meet this goal; the whole board cannot. It doesn't have the time. Occasionally, the informal nature of the collaboration between committees and the CEO might encourage a director to try to manage from the boardroom, but you can be on guard for that.

Ed Garden of Trian Partners argues that the compensation committee is the most important one on the board because it has the power to influence management behavior, which entails monitoring execution of company plans. He says, "We've seen so many situations where companies are underperforming, yet management is being paid a lot of money."

For example, Trian recently dug into the numbers of a big company in which it had become a major shareholder. Garden says, "The management team continued to miss their own targets and underperform versus peers, yet they were being paid above their target compensation level. And you scratch your head and say, like, why? How could the compensation committee come to that conclusion?"

For that reason, Garden sits on the compensation committee of every board he joins. He says, "I always make the point to the other board members, to management, to other shareholders that we're glad to pay management a lot of money if they build the business and do it the right way. But what we're not going to do is pay people just for showing up."

In such circumstances, the job of the compensation committee is to hold management to account. In the boardroom, when management presents slideshow comparisons of performance or the budget against the previous year, very rarely does it do so against the competition, and the directors don't have enough time to dig in and ask the right questions. Indeed, only a few board members will have any questions at all, and they are likely to ask them only here and there. Nobody wants to embarrass management.

This mindset must change. The committee must develop the depth of knowledge about the company's operations so that the full board is better prepared to make sense of management presentations, drawing on data both from inside the company and from the wider marketplace. In so doing, the committee will help the management team improve.

For instance, say a product launch turns out to have been better than budgeted. The committee should ask the CEO about the people who oversaw the launch. How is the company compensating them? The committee will then have more concrete knowledge about key talent. Or say a product design failed. Why did it fail? If the manager can answer that question, now the committee knows that this is a person who can understand and explain why something went wrong. The job of linking execution with key talent and their compensation can take place in this setting.

This committee should meet quarterly. If the directors on the committee evaluate performance four times a year, they will learn the business in depth. And that knowledge will give the company a competitive advantage. The board should survey management every year to evaluate the committee and show how useful it is.

The lead director should chair this committee. The best candidate is typically a former CEO—someone who has experience with transitions.

Strategy and Risk Committee

The central role of this committee will be to evaluate strategic options and alternate business models. These include the choice of goals and objectives; the competitive advantage of the company and its shelf life through the eyes of the customers; the possibilities for flexible response if conditions change; and the capabilities that the company will need for the future and the ones that it can discard.

To do its job, the committee must seek independent sources of information—about data, external trends, future scenarios, and competition—and should do so with the knowledge and help of the CEO. Jeffrey Ubben of ValueAct Capital and Inclusive Capital Partners says,

"Strategy is the domain of the whole board, but it cannot be done by the whole board. The committee has to prepare the way for the board because of the depth of work necessary to understand the external market, the competition, the key performance indicators, and the balance between short-term and long-term goals." The chairman of the strategy committee can be a member of the compensation committee and vice versa, so communication is straight, direct, and unfiltered.

Here the committee can learn about the projects and innovations that will build the future and the resources needed for them—the allocation of funds for those initiatives and the assignment of people. And it is here that the committee can evaluate risks and their possible causes, such as debt liquidity or the failure of an acquisition, as well as possible benefits, such as risk that enhances the market value of the company through acquisitions or new projects.

When such issues arise, the committee chair can ask management to present them for review. The committee can then seek external help to analyze them. By reevaluating strategy every quarter, a four- or five-member committee with a solid chair can take a forward-thinking look on resource allocation, future building, and risk.

On the composition of the committee, at least one or two members should come from outside the industry. If the company has a technology committee, it should have one member in common with the strategy and risk committee. People from inside the industry will have viewpoints that reflect the company's experience. Outsiders will bring an uncontaminated opinion. Diversity matters here—diversity of risk, of experience, and of skills. The strategy committee should also ask if the management team has a diverse perspective, and new people who can shake things up.

For example, in 2014, Providence Health of Seattle recruited a key Amazon employee, Aaron Martin, a senior manager of the Kindle division. At Providence, he would serve as senior vice president of strategy and innovation and supervise work on algorithmic and related technologies. The company also invited him to attend executive leadership meetings and encouraged him to ask questions and make suggestions that challenged the mindset of the existing team. He did, without fear that health-care insiders would consider some of his questions dumb.

Those questions began to alter the thinking of the leadership team and helped Providence assume the outlook of a digital player. Providence has since made huge strides toward its transformation into a data company, aligning with Microsoft and Amazon through large database acquisitions and creating alliances to get data from health-care companies and doctors. Martin is now chief digital officer and sits on the strategy committee of the board. The lesson: sometimes you have to bring along a disrupter to ask dumb questions when the old executive leadership people don't fully recognize what is possible.

After sitting together for a time, the strategy committee's presentations to the board should evolve. Rather than featuring five-year plans with a slew of numbers, they will express clear goals. They will offer an assessment of options, risk, implementation, and competitive advantage based on external factors—market data, customer information, technological trends, new players in the field. Focused presentations will help the rest of the board ask good questions about projects that the company is pursuing to build the future.

The strategy and risk committee will have cross-membership with the talent, compensation, and execution committee, which will help build value and balance short-term and long-term goals.

Audit Committee and Nominating and Governance Committee

These two old-line committees are both mandated by statute, but they also sit at a sensitive juncture between the board and management, of special significance at a time of rapid change and financial threat.

The audit committee does the heavy lifting on the oversight of financial risk. It has the authority to make decisions, and its work is evaluated publicly, giving it clear accountability. It has outside auditors, through which the committee will have access to independent, external sources of information, helping it correct the board's information deficit with management.

The audit committee is also one of the most demanding committees to serve on. Mary Erdoes of J.P. Morgan Asset & Wealth Management describes the requirements vividly. She says, "As head of the audit committee, you already have one of the most painful jobs in that we send you reams of paper every single month. And the audit committee meets more frequently than the rest of the board. And they have to go through every line of business and every audit. So that is a massively full-time job, especially as head of that committee."

The members of the audit committee also have to spend a good deal of time on the road to familiarize themselves with company operations. At J.P. Morgan, Erdoes says that the head of the audit committee flew to a different location almost every month. As she puts it, "He'd go to Japan. He'd hold town hall meetings with the people there. Then he'd meet with the Japanese regulators. Not every board member will have the time to do that, depending on the stage of their life, but boy, when they can, it's just like a totally different level of help for that company." In appointing the audit committee chair, look for someone who can make that investment.

In one respect, the nominating and governance committee is the pivotal committee of the board: the recruitment and dismissal of directors and the organization of the board and its committees are all within its ambit. Ideally it will have four members, all independent directors. We prefer each member to be the chair of another committee, which will ensure that the committee has the relevant information about all of the board's work.

The chair of the nominating and governance committee is of vital importance because of the committee's mandate over the leadership structure of the board. Just as the board prepares for succession of management, this committee must prepare for the succession of its own leadership, as well as the leadership of other committees and the board as a whole. It must search for directors before it needs them, drawing on its own network, the networks of other directors and the CEO, and headhunters. And it will need to plan at least three years in advance to ensure it has time to attract the right people for membership.

If it doesn't meet its recruitment goals in a way that adds value, the informal network of directors loyal to the CEO will seek to take on the committee's role. And if management selects the directors, the board will lose control of its independence. The key is whether the committee has the guts to make the right decisions, to establish the right processes, and to modify them as conditions change.

Today its centrality is heightened. Together with the audit committee, which is responsible for overseeing the management of liquidity, the governance committee is at the heart of one of the most sensitive dances with management, and one that will be of crucial importance in the postpandemic era.

In most circumstances, a bright line exists between the CEO and the board, dividing their separate responsibilities. For the board, the line means that the directors must not stray into the territory of management and attempt to run the company.

But some functions will straddle the line. For example, management may choose to focus on efficiency—the optimal use of resources to create long-term value. The board will properly focus on resiliency—enhancing survivability in times of stress and therefore instructing on necessary changes in priorities and capital allocation. And in so instructing, the board is straddling the bright line.

Yet here the board must do so, because it is accountable for priorities and capital allocation in times of risk. The top ten investors will ask the board questions about those matters. They will ask, for example, what priorities are you setting? What are you doing to enhance resiliency? What is your process for capital allocation? If you have a disagreement with the CEO, how do you deal with it?

A change in priorities and capital allocation can demand a change in key performance indicators and incentives for management. That is, the key performance indicators for resiliency will be very different from those for efficiency. That difference exists because the goals will be different. If your goal is efficiency, you will aim to maximize performance for earnings per share. If you change your goal to emphasize resiliency, you must now maximize performance for liquidity. (The rebalancing in performance indicators will also demand coordination with the strategy and compensation committees.)

Resiliency becomes a priority for the continuity of the business when volatility is high or at times of surprise, as with unexpected negative results. The response in those circumstances must be to avoid taking on too much debt or risk and to refrain from attempts to maximize earnings by skating on the edge.

In other words, the need to enhance resiliency is a continuous phenomenon of uncertainty, which can bring deep volatility and which will come unannounced, and in any number of forms—a transformational act of terror, a financial meltdown, a pandemic. In overseeing decisions about liquidity, and in adjudicating the lines of demarcation between the board and management at a time of great volatility, the audit and the nominating and governance committees must constantly refresh the knowledge and expertise of the board, making sure it has the right members for the demands of the day and the right balance between financial risk and reward.

Cybersecurity, Ad Hoc, and Temporary Committees

The board must have the flexibility to create and dissolve committees as the needs of the company change. For instance, Wendy's established a technology committee because it was transforming itself from a standard fast-food company to one with a digital ordering platform that would be essential to its operations. The company needed help in this transformation. In creating and staffing a technology committee, it had to decide whether it had directors who could understand the technological needs of the company. As an alternative, it would have to create or consult with an advisory group.

In speaking of the company's challenges, Ed Garden of Trian says, "We owned 20 percent plus of Wendy's, and we said to Wendy's management team, 'You may sell cheeseburgers for a living, but make no mistake, you're a technology company.' MobilePay, mobile ordering, the iPhone has changed everything about our business. So why not bring in technology expertise? And by the way, those people tend to be younger and probably not have the résumé that the search firm has historically pursued."

A technology committee could either be temporary or become permanent depending on the evolution of the relevant technology and the future needs of the company. The composition of the committee and its work could also change with the passing years.

Many companies used to have operating or executive committees of the board, but most have abandoned them because directors didn't like the two-tiered board structure that ensued. Don't dismiss the idea out of hand; circumstances may sometimes require such an approach. In its stead, one increasingly popular option is the temporary board task force. Vanguard recently used one to help with its strategy in a new country and another to develop a product for a market in which a couple of its directors had deep knowledge.

Companies are also using ad hoc committees to address rapid changes in their risk profiles, particularly in technology. Even more than vulnerability to a hack of their customers' personal information, what keeps CEOs awake at night is the risk of a catastrophic breach of the products themselves, as companies integrate more electronics into their goods and then bring them online. The CEO of one prominent *Fortune* 50 corporation says, "At first we were handling it in our risk committee, but we decided for a period of time to have a dedicated cybersecurity committee."

So, for many companies, the lineup of committees will be fluid, with some committees going out and others coming in. A company will always need new talent in the boardroom, as it does in its managerial ranks, because strategy must change as the business environment changes; otherwise the company will run significant risk. As new risks and strategies emerge, so will new committees.

CHECKLIST FOR REDESIGNING THE BOARD'S COMMITTEES

- Give critical responsibilities to board committees to overcome the information asymmetry with management.

- Let the lead director serve ex officio on all committees and appoint the committee chairs.

- Use committees to collaborate with the CEO and the management team in an informal setting.

- Be sure each committee has a clear twelve-month agenda that it shares with the whole board.

- Have the lead director or one of the committee chairs sit in on every committee meeting.

- Revamp the compensation committee to include responsibility for talent and execution.

- Give the strategy and risk committee primary responsibility for overcoming the asymmetry of information with management.

- Make sure that potential recruits to the audit committee have the time to invest in the job.

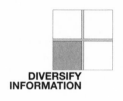

**DIVERSIFY
INFORMATION**

CHAPTER 6

Diversifying Information

I nformation is the lifeblood of the board of directors. Reducing the asymmetry of information between the board and management is essential to the board's mission of overseeing talent, strategy, and risk.

To oversee talent, the board must attain a deep understanding of the people who are setting the agenda for the company today and who'll be creating it for the future. Doing so means knowing the skills of the current team members, their bench strength as a source for the next generation of leaders, and the marketplace for talent outside the corporation.

To oversee strategy, the directors must know enough about trends in the industry to guide the company on the path toward long-term growth. They must learn the ins and outs of each of the company's lines of business so they can help management make informed decisions about which ones to nurture and which to exit, and when to proceed with a merger or acquisition and when to take a pass.

To oversee risk, the board must have a grasp of the perils of the marketplace today and the vulnerabilities of the company to forces that might rise to the level of existential threat. The board must also be able to judge the level of risk worth accepting in order to promote long-term growth.

All of these roles require the directors to have information unmediated by management; without it, they won't have perspective on what the CEO is telling them. And even though each member of the board might be independent in their mindset and values and courage, the board as a whole cannot be independent without its own sources of information, especially ones that reach outside of the corporation. Independence of information—its sources, selection, format, timeliness, frequency—is the basis for independence of judgment, intuition, thought, and action.

This imperative is not about databases or mass quantities of intelligence. It's about access to the information that matters—data that is relevant to the business of the corporation and that encompasses varied approaches to governance, from conservative to risk taking. The information must support strategic thinking from different perspectives, too, demanding not only diversity of age, gender, ethnicity, and experience on the board but also diversity of sources. And because the information landscape is changing so rapidly, boards must continually take note of new technologies and modes of analysis. The premium is on thinking that crystallizes quantities of information into qualitative statements.

Information independence is a matter for the committees as well as the whole board. As we've seen, give-and-take and the suspension of egos is easier in groups of four than in groups of ten, and the ensuing informality of discourse helps drive new ideas. So the deep work between managers and directors will take place in the committees. In that setting, directors can better clarify their expectations about the kind of information they want from management. Then the committees can sift and analyze the material and send their findings to the board.

In the course of tapping all sources of information to stay informed, board members may run into a sacred cow: thou shalt not trust external experts, especially ones who might take a view opposed to management's. But boards cannot rely solely on management for intelligence about the forces of change and disruption in the wider market. Sometimes the right questions are the awkward ones that come from outsiders, guiding the board into new avenues of research and analysis. At the same time, in developing alternative viewpoints, directors must always keep the CEO in the loop, as private equity companies do.

Still, as one expert after another told us for this book, it's the data advantage of managers over directors that imperils the work of the board. Directors who lack information may equate caution with safety, to the detriment of long-term planning.

The data gap means that the board can't easily challenge management when the company is going astray. If the CEO gives the board an explanation for disappointing execution, the board needs its own information sources so it can determine whether to adopt a different point of view. Indeed, look inside a company that is ailing, and you will often find a breakdown at the board level. As Ed Garden of Trian Partners puts it, "Companies are underperforming, and management is telling the board all the reasons it's not their fault. And the board doesn't know enough about the nuances and the subtleties of the business to push back. The information advantage that management has is the culprit."

With the directors in the dark, the board will struggle to play a useful role. Directors may wish to have meaningful discussions about strategy, but most don't understand the company or the industries well enough to do so. As a result, boards often don't know where to focus, so they engage in superficial discussions and interject unhelpful suggestions, leading to frustrating interactions between management and the board.

In this chapter, we'll offer ideas to help you and your fellow board members as you seek information both from outside the company and from your own management. And we will show you how some exemplary directors get the information they need, and the commitment that's necessary to do it. (See figure 6-1.)

FIGURE 6-1

The new value playbook: Information

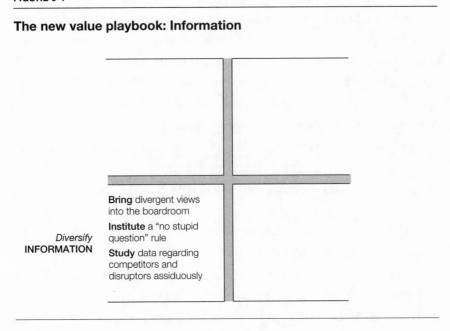

Diversify
INFORMATION

Bring divergent views into the boardroom

Institute a "no stupid question" rule

Study data regarding competitors and disruptors assiduously

Information from Management

One of the major challenges directors face is that management will often inundate them with information. At board meetings, the typical management presentation will consist mostly of historic data, which, besides eating up much of the session, inevitably skews the discussion toward short-term thinking. Management might not offer alternatives to its plans or discuss emerging trends, whether on public policy, technology, new competitors, or new models of operating.

To get much of that information, the board will have to go outside the company. But directors must still rely on management for information necessary to determine whether the company is well positioned for the long term. And that will require consultation and collaboration with the CEO and the management team.

The key managerial officer for this role is the CFO. The CFO should be the linchpin in generating the information that goes to the board.

Ideally, a single director or a committee will sit with the CFO and design the format for the information that will go to the board. The aim is to give the directors and their committees all they need to assess company strategy, including current news, planned initiatives, and internal analyses of the competitive landscape.

Common practice has been for management to slap together two-hundred-page reports and send them to the board. We think that this routine is a terrible practice. A page a week from management to the board should be sufficient. If any directors wish to know more, they can pick up the phone and call.

To help assess talent in the company, directors should spend time with a wide array of insiders. At Tyco International, Ed Breen would arrange dinners with a variety of executives and in-the-trenches staffers. He would also arrange for three or four directors to visit a company site on their own for a full day with the local management team and their staff, spending time on the factory floor or in the research labs. The directors would learn about not only the managers running the show but also the degree to which the local workforce is engaged with the long-term objectives of the company and how much it values the leadership.

The gold standard for how a CEO can help keep the board informed and give it an outside view is GM's Mary Barra. She is a firm believer that not all good ideas come from within the company or from its board members. So at least once a year, she has a buy-side and a sell-side analyst come in and make a presentation about the company on whatever subject they wish. Barra says, "We really try to be challenged with those who are aware of the industry and have different perspectives." Indeed, on our own boards, we like to bring in analysts whose outlook differs from ours to expose directors to alternative ways of thinking.

Barra tries to impart information with discipline, taking care to make good use of the board's time rather than burying directors with paper. At the urging of the board, she provides directors with a daily news digest summarizing coverage of GM and its competitors, offering both snippets and full articles for directors who want to read more. Once a month, the company also sends board members a public policy briefing because so much of what is happening in the industry has global policy and regulatory implications.

Before meetings, directors get a two-page brief laying out the issues of note and the decisions that management has made in response, along with a rundown of matters to be discussed at the meeting and the insights she'd like from the board. And she sends the board a collection of analyst reports every week. She says, "Sometimes you read them and as the CEO I cringe a little. But it's a perspective. And we make sure they're well rounded and have opposing views."

All this information is useful because it has been curated rather than delivered by the ton. And it's the sort of intelligence that can help the board add value going forward. Once it has comprehensive information relating to the competition, both on business matters and on talent, the board can make a real contribution by raising issues that management might not have considered. Barra says, "You have different board members who want to dig into certain areas more than others, either to learn more about the business or to deep dive into something. We try to be as time conscious as possible, but we probably overcommunicate a little bit, and then it's left to the board member how much they want to dig in."

Barra is lucky to have a board willing to spend the time necessary to keep abreast of issues, especially with a company in the midst of a long-term transformation. As a result, ideas flow in both directions. She says that rarely does a week go by when she doesn't receive at least one note from a board member about something that's happening to make sure she knows about it and to seek her perspective.

The care that Barra takes with her board's time raises an important point: true, directors should be well informed by management, and they should never be surprised. Yet they should also never have to search for a needle of insight in a haystack of verbiage. Vanguard's Jack Brennan recounts, "I just did a presentation for bank directors at the

Fed. And these poor guys are saying, 'I get a thousand pages for every board meeting. It just can't be valuable.'"

Often that sort of information dump is deliberately obfuscatory. Directors should resist it. CEOs sometimes use board meetings, too, as a way to hold directors at bay. Warren Buffett says, "If the CEO really wants to keep you under control—and there's been a half dozen in my experience—they'd basically just control the clock. They schedule presentations that don't tell you one damn thing about the business. And they use up the time, and they know when you want to get the hell out of there. A CEO that wants a puppet board can still get one, I'll put it that way."

The Activist Perspective

One of the signal characteristics of private equity is a tight alignment between managers and owners. The interest that activist investors take in public companies reflects that mindset. We think that public companies should do more to bring that attitude into their own arsenal of ideas.

To that end, boards should try to anticipate the information that a shareholder activist might seek out. To see the business as an activist would, Raj Gupta of Delphi Automotive asks outsiders to analyze the business and write a letter to management as if they were activist shareholders. The letter should be well documented, using external sources of information, and the tone should be realistically direct and hard-hitting. Such a perspective may embolden the board. In like manner, CEOs should invite one or more buy-side analysts to participate on all investor calls and have them ask questions. In the end, the aim of the directors and management will be the same: to create value for the long term.

Boards of private equity companies gather information because their livelihood depends on it. Public companies should act that way, too.

Buffett says, "Of the twenty public boards I've been on, only one, Data Documents, started as a private company. We went public, but when it was private, that's the best board I've ever been on. We held meetings at my house for a while, and we would go till three in the morning. And we wouldn't be doing one damn thing that would be required by the government or the New York Stock Exchange."

In our experience, activists can help you spot reasons for poor performance and vulnerability to takeovers. These investors are generally pretty smart and do very good analytical work. They start with the assumption that the company has underperformed relative to its peers. Then they look for reasons why this might be so. Is it due to poor management? Does the company have a portfolio that is overly complex and difficult to manage? Or does it have an underleveraged balance sheet?

Those factors divide analysts into P&L activists and balance sheet activists. The balance sheet activists will tell you to buy shares and pay a dividend and do it quickly. The others will point to the places you're underperforming because your costs are too high or your products are commodities or you need to simplify your portfolio. The implication is that if your management isn't capable of making the adjustment, then your stock will continue to languish. So boards must be almost ruthless in probing whether management is creating value for the long term. If not, they must take action before the activists come in.

We also like companies that look beyond management for ideas on how to develop skills needed for the future. Michele Hooper of the Directors' Council brings in a nominating advisory committee made up of outside investors and a clinician to help generate ideas for the skills matrix at UnitedHealth Group, on whose board she sits. She says, "We're an insurance company and a health-care company, and we talk about our long-term direction and the experience and skills we think we're going to need. And then we ask them for their input. Do you think we need to tweak it?"

Some people question why she would do something as scary as talk to her investors in that level of detail. Her experience is that the openness has yielded great insights and robust discussions about where the company is going. Other companies are going even further and are beginning to develop their own in-house universities. They are working with educational institutions to develop programs and curricula that will help give their entry-level workforce the sort of experiences that will be useful in the long term.

Outsiders can also help you see when your company is going astray. Among the first places we look to spot a breakdown in strategy or execution are analyst reports and board meetings with big investors. The board of one company we know—number three in its field—meets with investors every year, and management discusses its execution record for the period. Stating the specifics—the dollar amount invested in health care, say, or the number of positions eliminated in a stagnant division, or the percentage increase in cash flow—tells investors that the company does what it says it will do. But to get a good assessment of execution, the board should also hire an independent company to conduct meetings with customers. The objective would be to generate a net promoter score, a measure that is a proxy for the willingness of customers to recommend the company's products and that ranks the company against the competition.

The board can then see if the company has been improving or declining over time. The results will help you tell whether management is giving you the real reasons for the company's performance or is just making excuses. Beware if you hear management say, "We're doing all we can." Or "I've assigned the VP to do this." Or "this is a one-off mistake." Or "my regional manager died and we didn't replace him for two months." Or "it was an accounting mishap in China."

Having plenty of information to sift is one thing. How to make sense of it? Analysts and activists can help here, too. Sometimes it's not one big thing that spells trouble, but a lot of little things that begin to show a pattern. Former CA Technologies CEO and IBM executive Bill McCracken points out that with GE, no big red flag went up all of a sudden but rather a series of yellow flags over quite some time. He says, "Boards need to ask themselves a question: how many yellow flags make a red flag?"

At GE, the warning signs were there to see in the form of analyst reports that raised questions about revenue recognition and accounting principles and write-downs over a five-year period. McCracken says, "How many insurance companies exited the long-term-care insurance business before GE even declared that they had a big write-down coming at them?"

An example of a sharp outside perspective on GE's problems arrived in 2015, two years before Jeffrey Immelt stepped down as GE's CEO. Trian Partners issued an eighty-page white paper exemplifying how activists pull out facts in a way that managements and boards could, but typically don't—digging into the business, analyzing the numbers in depth against the competition, and arranging facts differently.

Among its findings: results at GE Capital completely offset the strong earnings growth of the industrial side of the business. The reason was GE Capital's very high capital intensity—a balance sheet item expressing the ratio of assets to sales. Management should consider capital intensity alongside gross margins—a profit and loss item. But Immelt never ran a balance sheet. GE totally missed that part of the equation. Getting rid of GE Capital did not free up capital to return to the shareholders. GE also overpaid for acquisitions. As a consequence, GE's ten-year compound annual growth rate was only 1 percent, and its total shareholder return over the period was only 10 percent—dead last among its peers. Gross margins were declining, too. Trian's conclusion: the reduced earnings per share and intensive use of capital caused GE's share value to decline by $11.20, or 45 percent.

If management has not already provided the board with the information necessary for this sort of analysis, the board must raise the issue in executive session and demand it—every detail of corporate performance versus the competition over time, in revenues, in margins, in EBITDA, benchmarked against the best and worst in the industry. If the company isn't able to provide that data, the board must seek it elsewhere. Otherwise, McCracken concludes, "That's where shareholders get very disturbed when they look back in the bright light of inspection. You say, 'Jeez, how did you miss that?'"

We believe that if the board takes the initiative to gather outside information for analysis and recommendations, the behavior of managers will change. They will think more broadly too, oriented toward the future. And when they assimilate a wider view, the need for outside checks should diminish. That modus operandi is how private equity works: the deal person always digs deep into the data on which the success of the business model depends. Public companies should do more to be as good as private equity in ferreting out and consuming information, aiming toward long-term results.

Wendy's is an example of how bringing in an outside viewpoint can help a company turn around and reorient toward long-term value. Around the time of the 2008 financial crisis, Wendy's got in trouble because it was trying to make quarterly numbers. And it did so by cutting the quality of its food, using cheaper buns, cheaper cuts of beef, cheaper condiments. It neglected its stores as well, forgoing upgrades.

Trian Partners had a 20 percent share in Wendy's at the time and helped engineer a turnaround. Ed Garden of Trian recalls, "We went in there and said, 'Stop the madness. We're going back to basics.'" Wendy's then improved the ingredients of the burgers and the condiments and began renovating the stores, putting in flat screens and Wi-Fi and fireplaces.

Trian's involvement, and the size of its stake, helped the company deal with shareholders. As Garden puts it, "We gave management cover to stop worrying about the next quarter and start worrying about 2025." Indeed, the stock was stagnant from 2009 to 2012. The shareholders said, "We don't care about the improvements; the stock hasn't moved." Garden responded, "We believe the stock will move as we build the business." The shareholders would make five times their money.

To us, it's a prime example of how a long-term private equity mindset can help companies in the public realm. Smart companies will emulate them. Shelly Lazarus, former CEO of Ogilvy & Mather, likes to talk to analysts and investors without management present. She found that the matters on which they focused were different from the ones that would arise if she were meeting with only her fellow directors, so for her, the encounters were eye-opening. She says, "I've become a huge advocate of listening to investors and shareholders, which I don't think is part of the best practice for boards even today."

But even if they have no position in the company, activist investors are worth talking to because they can give the board a good take on the company's strategy versus the behavior of the broader marketplace. State Street's Ron O'Hanley speaks vividly of a conference in which he asked the attendees to imagine that he was an activist investor and that they were on the board of Pfizer. "I come in and I say to you, would you like my opinion as to how your strategy stacks up against that of Eli Lilly?" recalls O'Hanley. "You can see that the CEOs in the room had a look of sheer horror on their faces. But the board members all sat up straighter, thinking, oh, that would be great." The lesson: outsiders who make managers a little bit nervous can help directors generate novel strategic options.

How Directors Can Take the Lead

Getting your hands on the information you need involves more than commissioning reports and inviting outsiders to address the board. To be a good director, and to get up to speed, you have to invest your personal time in addition to the time you spend at board meetings. Good CEOs will invite their boards to customer events, exhibitions, and dinners where directors can see their company's products, mingle with their workforce and clientele, and hear how both groups view the company; the same holds true for annual investor events.

Directors must take advantage of such opportunities. They will gain multiple insights into the company from different perspectives—from investors, customers, external advisers, experts. Far from simple social- izing, in those settings you will see the company's position in the com- petitive landscape, along with the trends that will affect the industry in the years ahead.

Directors should also be ready to broaden their scope beyond the customary ways of analyzing company operations. For instance, in reviewing performance data, they should seek out more than the standard metrics of market share, margins, and profitability. In order to assess performance related to talent, Lady Lynn Forester de Rothschild, CEO of E.L. Rothschild and cofounder of Inclusive Capital Partners, has focused on employee retention levels versus her company's peers. She says, "These are hard-to-get comparables, but we do ask that from our managers to show us how we keep people." Great CEOs now also measure diversity in the lower ranks.

In our view, the job of directors is to make sure that such input doesn't come only through management's filter. In this regard and others, the Directors' Council's Michele Hooper is unparalleled as a director, both dedicated and meticulous. She doesn't just read reports; she observes, collects information over time, and gets the touch and feel of the companies where she's a director.

Hooper explains that in the normal course of events, directors will hear from the CEO and the management team about their vision of the industry and where the company is going. She says, "To me, that's one data set, and it's not sufficient. As a board member, I'll call it the starting point. And that's why you have to go out and do your own homework."

So instead of relying on management, Hooper goes to conferences on her own, where she can learn about new directions in, say, technology and big data and disruptive competitors—issues that directors from many companies are dealing with. While she's on the road, she will talk to these colleagues to get a sense of new research she might wish to understand.

Hooper is unusual in the initiative she brings to her boards. She says, "I view my board work as a profession. My job isn't simply to get the board books and talk to the person in the company who's dealing with issue X. I also view it as my responsibility to do my own competitor analysis." All directors might wish to adopt her approach to the job as they seek to create value for the long term.

CHECKLIST FOR DIVERSIFYING INFORMATION

- Tap external experts to help you assess management's explanation of performance.

- Obtain news, planned initiatives, and internal analysis of the competition to help you assess company strategy.

- Resist management information dumps; have them send you brief updates every month.

- Benchmark your customer satisfaction against your competitors' performance to gauge management's explanation for performance.

- Demand that management provide you with every detail of corporate performance versus the competition over time. Compare with analyst reports.

- Meet with analysts and investors without management in the room.

- Take advantage of opportunities to meet with your company's workforce and clientele.

- Focus on metrics like employee retention versus the competition as well as standard metrics of market share, margins, and profitability.

- Go to conferences on your own and talk to fellow directors there to get a sense of new research you might want to tap into.

ENGAGE INVESTORS

CHAPTER 7

Engaging with Investors

A quarter of a century ago, corporate power rested in the hands of the imperial CEO, who might simply tell you to dump your stock if you didn't like what he was doing (and it would always be a "he"). Since then, long-term investors and activists have taken the stage and, along with market forces, are now holding boards to account. In managing their company's talent, strategy, and risk, and especially in planning for the long term, boards must also manage the relationship with investors, their most powerful constituency.

This boardroom mandate is essential because investors—especially a company's permanent shareholders—are collectively the primary driver behind the new TSR. These investors are demanding that companies abandon the practices that encourage pursuit of short-term gains—such as compensation structures skewed toward stock market performance and acquisition strategies designed only to buy revenues. A quick hit in the market does nothing for a long-term investor, especially if it hampers opportunities for strategic moneymaking initiatives.

Index funds can't apply leverage to management by threatening to sell their stock; they buy shares and hold them in perpetuity. Instead, these investors are seeking influence in boardrooms. And their aim is to refocus the attention of management on a different set of priorities—on long-term planning; on improvements in execution; on talent, strategy, and risk.

This relationship between companies and investors is sometimes collaborative and sometimes adversarial, and knowing which way the compass will point is not always an obvious matter. For that reason, the attitude of board members to investors is often wary and watchful and, in the case of activist investors with their frequent pressure for short-term gains, outright distrustful.

We can tell you that distrust is not an action plan. Investors are not created equal—even activists. All have their own objectives. Each will have a frame of reference and a model of investment, and no two investors will have exactly the same one. They collect different information and have different ways to diagnose it and different objectives. Boards must learn what their model is.

In dealing with investors, you must also keep in mind that the failure of an investment has a greater impact on the income of an investor than on the income of a board member and a greater impact on the investor's reputation, too. If directors fail—if the board fails—they may dent their reputation but lose very little money. The investor loses their paycheck and the ability to raise funds in the future. It's the investors, not the directors, who take the loss. So do all that you can to understand the criteria on which investors base their decisions and conceive of their risk.

Investors are almost always smart, often with insights about your company and its competitors. Think of your investors—your owners—as a resource. Whether or not they are hostile to your long-term objectives, they have information that can help you and that is worth getting, no matter their aims.

We can help you decide how to manage this relationship productively—how to meet with investors, and when; how to get their useful

FIGURE 7-1

The new value playbook: Investors

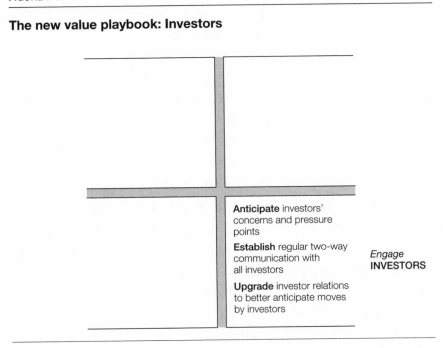

Anticipate investors' concerns and pressure points

Establish regular two-way communication with all investors

Upgrade investor relations to better anticipate moves by investors

Engage
INVESTORS

feedback; how to understand what each type of investor is looking for; and how to deal with activists. And we will show you what one major activist looks like up close. (See figure 7-1.)

Meeting with Investors

Some boards resist talking to investors, leaving the job to management. We believe meeting with investors is an essential responsibility of the board. As we saw in chapter 6, investors can be an independent source of the critical information that boards need so that they know as much as management does and can plan for long-term value. Smart boards are engaging with investors to redress this asymmetry of information.

Take the example of Estée Lauder Companies, which had a policy that discouraged directors from talking directly with investors. The rationale for the policy was that management was already spending a lot of time and resources on investor engagement. Not too long ago, Vanguard asked to have a meeting with the head of the board's compensation committee. The board went back and forth about whether to take up the invitation. Finally it did.

For Lady Lynn Forester de Rothschild, who sits on the Estée Lauder board, the meeting was an eye-opener. The head of the compensation committee was able to bring back to the board some insights that management hadn't shared with it about its own interactions with investors. She says, "I was skeptical of board engagement with institutional investors, but I now think it is a really good idea for both sides. It's one that makes management, for obvious reasons, nervous. But I think we should try to do as much of it as the investment community wants."

Engaging with big shareholders can help you identify which are in it for the long term and which might align with activists. The big challenge is short-termism—the pressure to make a quick profit. So often, doing so will not be in the best long-term interest of the company. That is why the issue of shareholder engagement is so important. The point at which an activist arrives is not the time you want to inform and educate your major investors about your story and your strategy.

A clear rationale for what you're doing and what to expect can also keep activists at bay even if your strategy is atypical for your industry. When Raj Gupta, current chair of Aptiv, was on the board of Tyco International, the activist fund Relational Investors took a position in the company. Gupta says, "They came out and met with Ed [Breen, the chairman] and CEO George Oliver, and they walked away and sold their position in three months. They said, 'You guys are doing just about everything we would do.'"

Communicating clearly with investors can keep them on your side when you stumble. If you do what you promise, you'll get a pass for hiccups that might occur along the way.

What investors want to know

When you meet with investors, they are likely to ask questions designed to expose your vulnerabilities—operational, financial, and competitive. They will also be probing the effectiveness of your measures for overseeing the management team. Their aim is to ensure that you are managing talent, strategy, and risk to enhance shareholder return. But whether they are angling for a short-term gain or long-term value will depend on the investor.

For some players—index funds and activists, say—you may know their frame of reference going in, and you can tailor your preparation for meeting with them accordingly; for others, you might only learn about their agenda when you hear what they want to know. But in all cases, the work you do to prepare for their questions can also help you crystallize your plans for creating long-term shareholder return.

Among the most critical questions you will face from investors are those focusing on how the board ensures that management isn't making short-term decisions that hamper value creation. They will seek to know whether the directors—collectively and individually—subject management to sufficient levels of scrutiny or whether they tend to give management a pass.

To prepare for these questions, you have to think like an investor, which necessitates candor in sizing up your fellow board members. In assessing the performance of former CEOs on boards, Dan Riff of Advantage Solutions looks to see whether they bring the same level of expertise and urgency to their board work that they did when they were running their own company in a way that created value for Advantage's clients. He says, "Sometimes they retire from CEO roles where they were amazing and settle back a bit on the board and rubber-stamp a lot of what the others are doing. When was the last time the board really got in the field and got its hands dirty with upper-middle management?" If the answer is anything other than "recently," the board isn't doing its job.

Investors may also ask how the board prepares for succession, both in the company and on the board itself, and how it ensures that the company is building the capabilities it will need for long-term growth. To that end, investors will want to know how the board develops its own sources of information so it can make independent judgments about the market for talent. After all, if the directors don't have independent information, how can they ask the right questions?

You should be ready to explain the logic of the CEO's compensation as well. The level of pay, along with the types of compensation and the trigger for enhanced rewards, will tell investors whether the company is emphasizing short-term or long-term growth, or keeping the two in balance. For instance, annual bonuses and rewards often go up when the stock rises. But if the CEO gets a 200 percent bonus for exceeding the targeted share price, that's a driver of short-termism. If management pulls money from the future to meet short-term goals, investors will want to know if the managers must first seek board approval.

To get a handle on what the board is doing to manage talent, strategy, and risk, investors will look to see how the board is spending its time. What are the biggest debates at the board level? Are they about procedural issues or truly focused on strategic opportunity and risk? How do directors think about the holes on the board? What skills does the board lack as the business is evolving? How much time do directors spend on each important matter in their purview? Is the board engaging with outside experts to help make decisions on large capital allocations?

Investors will ask stakeholder questions, too. What has the board done to help the company be a good corporate citizen, to promote diversity in the company's ranks, to respond to climate change and the possibility of requirements for zero-carbon initiatives?

Investors may ask how the board thinks about metrics. In most companies, management sets the metrics by which the company tracks value creation. Does the board ever question them or ask management to change them? Whether you speak to the question or not, investors are going to spend time poring over your proxy statements, which may give insight into the metrics that the board considers along with incentives and ownership levels in the company.

The lesson: you should be sure to know as much about your company as your investors do.

When to meet with investors and what to tell them

Boards meet with investors to get the benefit of their information and their analysis, but the same research will support different feedback depending on the investors' objectives. Still, some principles will govern the ways in which you establish a relationship with any of them.

A key imperative of the engagement is having regular meetings. Creating a relationship with an investor takes time; you want to solidify that relationship before you need their help. Former Xerox CEO Anne Mulcahy would aim to meet the top twenty or thirty investors every eighteen months to two years. She says, "The intent is to have a regular cadence so that you can actually have relationships. It's both listening and sharing messages that you'd like them to hear on issues that are critical to the board." She also recommends meeting with any sizable investor who has requested engagement with the board. Mulcahy says, "Try to say yes 99 percent of the time."

Pacing, though, is important if you wish to keep major investors engaged instead of crushed by information overload. Shelly Lazarus, former CEO of Ogilvy & Mather, recalls a conference call with major investors across the country. Speaking to the representative of a state pension fund, a BlackRock rep said, "You're inundating us with information. We can't handle that level of interaction."

The takeaway: if every management team of every publicly traded company takes as best practice the need to reach out to every major investor, the investors will be overwhelmed. So when contacting an investor, be cognizant of their time constraints. Be focused. Lazarus's observation: "Know what you want to get out of the meeting. Know why you're having it. Know the value of the interaction."

For that reason, some investors advise taking a lighter approach to shareholder meetings. Daniel Pozen of Wellington Management says, "I wouldn't prescribe boards to interact on a regular basis with all sets of shareholders. It would be responsible practice for a board to invite one shareholder per year to give a presentation on their perspective of the company." The shareholders should rotate. Perhaps one year it could be a passive shareholder, and another year a long-term active shareholder, and then perhaps a former shareholder who exited for a certain reason, and the next time a shareholder with a medium-term time frame.

What to make of these varied opinions? Tailor your approach to the investor and be honest with yourself about the position of your company. Know that the desire of investors to meet with a board, and the frequency of the meetings, will be a function of your company's size and the size of their investment.

Who should take the meeting?

We propose that the part of the board best prepared to engage with investors is the talent, compensation, and execution committee. In our model of board committees, the chair of the strategy and risk committee would also be on the talent, compensation, and execution committee. Thus, it's the one place on the board where talent, strategy, and risk all converge.

Before members of any committee sit down with investors, be sure they are very well prepared. Nothing creates a worse impression on investors for board members to show up at a meeting clueless and ill-informed instead of fully briefed.

Directors should not overreach in what they disclose to investors. While the board should have open lines of communication with investors, the key person in the company to tell shareholders about important information is the CEO. How much should companies disclose? The best practice is to be transparent and then meet your commitments—do what you say you're going to do, even if it isn't a particular investor's favored strategy. For instance, GM has a diverse investor base, with widely different time horizons. The company tries to manage the relationship with each investor, but always doing what it believes to be the right thing for long-term shareholder value.

But since communication is a two-way street, GM's Mary Barra recommends openness to ideas from any investor. She says, "The first thing we do when we get a suggestion from an investor is ask, 'Hey, is this a good idea? Let's go research this.'" After every earnings call, she reaches out to a wide variety of GM's top investors but also to hedge funds with a short-term focus, and she tries to listen to all of them. She usually participates on three or four of those calls, and the head of investor relations and the CFO do so as well.

Those calls have led GM to undertake some new initiatives, especially on environmental issues, with the company adopting a more cohesive and comprehensive set of sustainability goals. Gathering good feedback is a great way to take advantage of your quarterly earnings call.

Warren Buffett also counsels openness with investors. Indeed, he believes that he should tell stockholders as much about what's on his mind as he would share with his two sisters if the three of them owned the company together—what things were worrying him, what the businesses were worth and why, how durable their competitive advantage was in one company versus the others, how he would allocate capital in the future.

Buffett says, "The CEO absolutely owes that to the owners. I have a strong feeling that everybody's entitled to the same information, and that means the important information about valuation prospects, and personnel, if it's important—exactly what you would tell somebody who was your silent partner if you had a two-person business." If that job is being done inadequately, he believes the directors ought to say so. He has no problem if people want to talk to his directors about whether he's living up to what he says or whether there are issues that he just doesn't get.

But he wouldn't delegate that job down the line. He says, "The person who's going to be responsible for the assets and how they're managed over time is the CEO, and you really want to hear from that person. And you don't want somebody else writing the report for them. I do not want some investor relations department pulling up a report with a lot of information that's not important."

In other words, it's not the board's role to disclose anything material about company financials or plans for the future. That's a job for management. It's fair for directors to tell investors how they oversee talent, strategy, and risk, and the management team, too. But the board's main task is to find out what investors think of the company and what they know about it.

Should you give guidance?

One of the thorniest issues companies face in dealing with investors is whether or not to give guidance. Our advice: don't do it. Or if you must, leave yourself plenty of leeway. Anything else is a fool's game. We agree with T. Rowe Price, which gives no guidance to its shareholders because it can never be sure what the numbers are going to be. Former chair Brian Rogers says, "As a public company ourselves, we avoid the guidance business like the plague. Companies and managements always want to underpromise and overdeliver, but all too often management teams get caught up in the overpromise because it feels good in the short term. And then if you disappoint, there's hell to pay."

Rogers recalls that some years ago, the CFO of J.P. Morgan was in the office, and his company was pushing for more guidance. The CFO said, "Look, all I can tell you is we have a return on equity objective, and you know what our book value is, so you guys figure it out." That was the extent of the guidance—a figure with a huge band around it where the likely outcomes would be. And that's really as far as you should go.

Guidance isn't often very useful for anyone, either. If a stock goes down because of a nonstructural issue, the price will usually bounce back soon, because its ten biggest shareholders—all of them long term—will own at least 50 percent of the shares. The rest will be in the hands of activist traders, and they have to react. But withholding guidance will change the behavior of analysts, and it will change their advice.

Guidance promotes short-termism. If companies can get out of the guidance business, or at least make guidance very long term, they would give themselves more room to follow long-term objectives.

How to Deal with Activists

For companies looking to manage for the long term, activist investors can pose a special threat, especially those who take a sizable position in your stock and press for a quick hit. Our advice: be on guard for the worst, but don't assume activists are the root of all evil. And even when their goals are misguided, they can be a fount of information.

In our experience, activists do much more extensive analytical work than any other player to identify the deficiencies of a company's strategy and structure with the aim of creating a higher market value for the shareholder. They might invest millions of dollars to consult experts and interview former and current employees, suppliers, and customers to assess a company's performance versus its competitors and to identify weaknesses and vulnerabilities. (See chapter 6 for an example of Trian Partners' work on GE.) You might not want to act on the analysis as an activist would; doing so could compromise your long-term objectives. But activists do get to the bottom of performance issues.

So as you meet with these investors, be prepared to learn from their questions. We have found that their diagnosis of company problems is often superior to the work done by the CFO and outside investment bankers, whose research is often driven largely by statistics rather than by real-world interviews. The board should pay close attention as activist investors probe and discuss their analysis with the CEO. The goal may be bad, but the opinion good. Use it.

Activists also invest resources in evaluating portfolios and mergers and acquisitions. You should be prepared for their inquiries. A typical metric that activists might research is how many of your acquisitions have created value and how many have destroyed it. While your board cannot tell the investor what it will be doing in the future, the investor will consult public information about performance of your past deals.

So in asking questions, the activist is seeing whether your answers gibe with its research. In other words, it is trying to tell how solid the board is and whether it has the necessary skills. Any conversation between investors and the board will have this question lurking just beneath the surface.

What type of activist is it?

Activists themselves come in different stripes, and you need to separate one from the other. Some have no particular orientation; some will want to break apart your portfolio; and some will try to create opportunities for a merger and achieve a new market value. The latter assume that many companies have businesses that do not belong; if they sold such assets to someone else, they would create more value at the unit's new home and derive more value themselves.

If you're judicious, you should be able to divide activists into these different camps and identify those that aren't out for a quick hit. Firms like T. Rowe Price and Wellington Capital Group think a lot like long-term investors and can offer insight that will help companies create value for the future.

The greatest threat comes in dealing with activists with a short time horizon. Jack Brennan, formerly of Vanguard, says, "They may be a sugar high for Vanguard's index assets, but they've got a one-, two-, three-year internal rate of return. You know the activist is there for a cup of coffee. And that's part of the biggest disruptive aspect of their presence."

Smart companies do what they can to deal with issues that might make the company vulnerable to an activist investor. For instance, though liquidity is important at a time of crisis, you must balance your need for emergencies against the risk of carrying too much cash on your balance sheet.

The irony is that sometimes management will try to inoculate the company against an activist attack by anticipating investor pressures. As Ed Garden of Trian Partners puts it, "When we go on the board, what we find is that management is the one that is short-term focused. They've been conditioned by the market to think short term. And we're the ones going in there and saying, 'Stop imagining. Let's plan and not get stuck in what was 2018.'"

Some investors trace the pressure for short-termism not to activists but to asset owners—institutions like pension funds, sovereign wealth funds, and endowments and foundations. ValueAct Capital's Jeffrey Ubben says, "They view private equity as their highest-return money but locked up and illiquid, and use public markets as their hyper-liquidity balance. Asset owners have shortened up the public market's time horizon."

This observation gibes with our experience in serving on public boards. One of our colleagues who sits on both public and private boards describes the difference between the two like this: "On the private boards I'm on, we have the agility to make changes whenever we need to, but we're thinking long term. On the public boards, we're thinking quarter to quarter, but we have no agility to make the changes that we need to." Try to assimilate the kind of long-term thinking you would find on private boards. When you do, you'll be thinking like an activist.

When activists make a move

If activists take a position in your company, engage them so they can understand your objectives. You can't decide who owns you, but you can affect the nature of the conversation.

Though many activists would not want to wait through long periods of poor performance before moving in on an undervalued stock, most hostile suitors don't act alone. Instead, they will seek the support of one or more big institutional investors. The top ten investors are likely to own 50 percent of the shares of the company. No activist can succeed in splitting up a company or taking out its board or CEO without the support of these large investors.

So the best way to defend against activists who are in it for the short term is to keep your large investors close to you. The board and the CEO must focus on communication with critical investors and persuasion to keep them on their side. What we're seeing now is that these large institutional investors prefer to use "friendly activism." They do extensive research and have a point of view they want to share with you, and their main concern is the company's longevity.

Whatever their goals, though, listening is the best approach in dealing with activist investors. Sometimes you might want to take advantage of their ideas. When Xerox's Anne Mulcahy was on the board of Target, activist investor William Ackman, whose Pershing Square owned 10 percent of the company, approached with proposals for restructuring. The board heard him out. Mulcahy recalls, "I think everyone would agree that this is not something you ignore. He had one good idea, which was to sell our financing arm, and we did it."

The lesson: assume that all investors can be a source of analysis and judgment. A lot of them have more of an owner mindset than many board members. Make such investors independent information partners.

When activists join the board

If an activist takes a seat on the board, what should you anticipate? How should you behave? Whatever your expectations, the best policy is to be a good listener and judge them by what they are saying, even if you don't like how they are saying it. Sometimes you might want to consider inviting an activist to join even if they can't force you to, especially if they demonstrate a genuine interest in long-term growth and a constructive point of view.

For instance, in some cases, activists come onto the board when the fundamentals of the company are not working and you need to make a change. A prime example is the move that Ubben made after his company bought a big stake in Microsoft. In 2013, he used his clout to place ValueAct's president on the Microsoft board and edge out Steve Ballmer as CEO. The move came after a failed strategy that saw Microsoft spend $7.2 billion to buy Nokia's phone business, among other bad bets. The change helped set Microsoft back on course.

Such upheavals can be traumatic, even if in the end they work for long-term value. Look at what an activist investor like Nelson Peltz, a founder of Trian Management, does when he arrives at a company in which he makes a big investment. Typically Trian will set up one of its most knowledgeable industry partners in a war room and insist on visiting and meeting with layers of management. This level of engagement can rattle existing board members. But the expertise that Trian injects can generate better questions for a CEO. The objective is to encourage board members to go beyond the meeting cadence and get their hands dirty.

So keeping an open mind when an activist joins the board can help you create value for your company. In 2013, after Trian took a position in DuPont, the investors sat down with the chemical maker and focused on the three things in the activist playbook: the cost structure, which is a proxy for operating efficiency and corporate governance; the capital structure, to assess whether the balance sheet is underleveraged; and the portfolio, to see if the business lineup is bloated and needs trimming. An idea that Trian proposed early on: to split the company in three. And the firm presented DuPont with a detailed, comprehensive analysis, over forty pages in length.

But according to former CFO Nick Fanandakis, Trian's numbers were way over the top. He says, "They said we could cut $2 to $4 billion from overhead costs. Well, we only had $4 to $5 billion in costs. So it was hard to swallow." What followed was a conflict that raged for two years. Trian made its white paper available to the investment community, and DuPont spent much time and money defending its own interpretation.

DuPont narrowly won a proxy fight, but six months later, after a downturn in its agricultural business, things heated up again, the CEO left, and Ed Breen, a board member, took over. Eventually DuPont would combine with Dow, realign their collective businesses, and split into agriculture, specialty, and commodity companies—an amalgam of Trian's original suggestion for a break-up and DuPont's for a straight-up merger with Dow.

The transformation of DuPont from a conglomerate to a trio of focused businesses would unlock tremendous value. Among the most productive ideas after Breen took over was jettisoning DuPont's matrix structure—which dated back four decades—in favor of one based strictly on lines of business. That change led to both direct and indirect savings. Fanandakis says that as soon as the businesses had costs under their control, they were more critical of their expenditures. The effect dominoed and led to greater savings than the shift from the matrix alone. In all, DuPont shaved $1 billion from annual costs—just a portion of what Trian said it would save, but still a windfall.

Looking back to those early days with Trian, Fanandakis says, "Our biggest mistake is that because the information they hit us with was so extreme in the first meetings, we hunched our shoulders and went into battle. If we were going to do it tomorrow, I wouldn't have been so defensive." Instead, he would have tried to be collaborative—to show Trian where its numbers were wrong and his were right, and to seek a more measured course of action that would benefit the company and the investor alike. In the end, the boardroom presence of this activist helped DuPont cut expenses, improve its capital structure, and revamp its portfolio, all to the benefit of long-term shareholder value.

Dealing with a destructive activist

Some activists will live up to your worst nightmares and, at the very least, bring a different sort of energy to the room. Vanguard's Brennan argues that with some exceptions, having an activist on the board changes the dynamic for the worse. He says, "The market should be the force that ensures that boards and management teams are as productive and cost effective and driven to succeed as they can be, which is why they need to get strategy and talent and risk management correct. Having a person with an agenda—that's different. The activist takes advantage of an aberration or creates an aberration to be disruptive."

An activist on the board can be destructive in their conduct as well. Shelly Lazarus, former CEO of Ogilvy & Mather, believes tone and behavior count for a lot in the boardroom, and that some activists seem to have gone to a class in how to be confrontational in the most aggressive way. She says, "I think the content of what activists bring is really important, but you don't necessarily have to have that kind of provocation. If they do insist on coming on the board and the company accedes to it, then behavior does matter. Being constructive does matter. It doesn't make a board more effective when you have somebody throwing fire bombs every half an hour."

If an activist does join your board, you might face obsession with minor details and, depending on the type of company you have, a double standard as well. State Street's Ron O'Hanley recalls the nitpicking and skepticism that Ford CEO Mark Fields encountered despite having what now looks like a pretty good plan, versus the pass that investors were giving Elon Musk when he was talking about Tesla. O'Hanley says, "Not everybody's a disruptor. We may be asking different questions, but we should have the same level of scrutiny. We let the disruptor get away with the conceptual charts, and we're boring away at the incumbent, looking at spreadsheet line g42 and saying why is it x as opposed to $1.2x$?" If you have an old-line company, an activist who moves in can be a challenge.

Still, even the most challenging relationships can bear fruit, as one novice CEO learned from his relationship with the most challenging activist of all. The lesson he would learn: be open, but don't be afraid to stick to your guns.

Thinking Like an Activist

In chapter 2, we saw that one of the board's main roles is to probe how well management does in introducing new products, rebalancing existing lines of business, and making acquisitions. And if it does this job rigorously, the board will be conceiving strategy as an activist would. Throughout the year, at every strategy meeting, as board members question management about new large-scale opportunities, they should always keep activists in mind, helping management strike the right balance between short-term and long-term planning and between the company's various stakeholders.

The board must be the driver of long-term thinking. Annual investment to build the future is imperative. Boards can take any number of steps to help create a longer-term perspective—say, by adopting an eight-quarter plan instead of a four-quarter plan, with a review of milestones every quarter. If a company invests for the future and short-term performance dips, the only real short-term risk is vulnerability to a takeover. Boards must have the backbone to understand why managers might be pressed to emphasize the short term and back them in taking a longer view.

The CEO's role in striking this balance is to be aware of all the pressure points and opportunities that activists might identify, and to discuss them with the board. Activist shareholders do their homework. They may exaggerate when they approach management and the board, but the gap between performance and opportunity is often real and well documented. They use McKinsey, former CFOs, and chief executives to advise them, and they can afford the expense, which will be small compared to their investment and potential gain.

Activists analyze companies in a number of different ways. They will look at a company's capital structure, as Trian did with GE in 2015 before declaring that the company had room for an additional $20 billion in debt to fund growth. Activists also look at cost structure—not just operating cost but marketing cost as well.

Legacy companies tend to see sales, general, and administrative costs as one item, whereas digital companies separate out sales costs and consider it a growth investment. These companies can measure efficiency by comparing their sales expense as a percentage of revenues against their peer group. For example, sales and marketing expense at software company Citrix was 40.3 percent of revenue in 2014—well above the industry average. Activists stepped in the following year.

Activists look at company portfolios, too. Among the questions an activist will ask: If a company has unrelated businesses, does each piece perform better than its peers? Do management claims of synergy translate into dollars and cents? Would any of the pieces be more valuable to somebody else? Managers of diversified companies sometimes allocate cash from a healthy business to a sick business. Sears did so in the 1980s and 1990s and failed to invest enough in IT, which was the linchpin of Walmart's success.

To avoid luring activists, beware of holding excess cash. Activists look for capital allocation in the form of cash. In the digital age, a high proportion of capital investment is operating expenditure. So a company needs a strategy that lays out how it will generate and assign cash for a minimum of three to five years.

Many companies have become net cash generators, and rates on borrowing are near zero. In the absence of credible plans to use the cash for growth and acquisitions, management may be tempted to use the money for share buybacks and dividends. The board must be vigilant to ensure that share buybacks decrease the number of shares outstanding. Otherwise, something is likely to be wrong, as when an overly large portion of compensation is in the form of stock options, which dilute the shares and suppress stock price. BlackRock CEO Larry Fink leveled this criticism in a letter to CEOs—too many dividend increases and buybacks in lieu of business growth.

Activists look for companies that are slow to adapt to the digital age. Digitization is transforming businesses, and some legacy companies are not moving quickly enough. Common laggards are brick-and-mortar retail stores, where a decline in store traffic is accelerating. A legacy company might think annual growth of 15 percent is fabulous and miss an adjustment for a structural decrease in total store sales.

Activists look for undervalued stock as well. The market may not recognize the potential of a company's strategy or the value of new initiatives for near- and long-term performance, perhaps because management credibility is low. The board must create allies in the investment community to make sure that management has support for well-founded long-term plans.

One trend that is helping insulate companies is a change in the structure of investments. Brennan of Vanguard says, "Market share gains by indexed investors is a huge win for governance and for corporate performance over time. The ultimate state of grace would be to have a large portion of your stock held by indexed investors who have a very real interest in the long-term success of your company, while also getting shorter-term feedback from the active world."

Throughout, the role of directors is to build credibility with investors. In so doing, the board should help managers devise a way to meet quarterly performance milestones as they invest to build the company's future. Before investor calls, coach the CEO to give investors detailed information and head off sell-side questions such as "What is the next quarter's tax rate?" Connect the long term and short term when responding to investors' questions. The board should watch for defensiveness on the part of management and within the board. Listen carefully to investor calls, not only the ones for your company but also for a selected peer group.

Smart companies use their investor day as an exercise in how to talk about their strategy. For instance, J.P. Morgan holds a full-day conference for investors every year, covering every line of business, and managers spend three months preparing for it, grilling themselves and asking questions that they might face in front of a big crowd. Each division must boil down those three months of work into a thirty-minute presentation.

In preparing for the conference, Mary Erdoes, in her role as head of J.P. Morgan Asset & Wealth Management, asks her staff to "tell me the truth, nothing but the truth, so help me God." She says, "There's nothing like it. I haven't figured out a way to get my people to feel the pain that I feel because they don't have to sit up in front of an entire audience of every analyst in the world, in addition to your regulators and your other lines of business. So you prep like nothing else." That time will pay dividends.

The Alpha Activist:
What a Close Encounter Can Tell You

Of all the activists who have engaged with public companies, the most renowned—or notorious, depending on your point of view—is Carl Icahn, whose fame as a corporate raider dates to the 1980s, with his hostile takeover of Trans World Airlines.

Icahn made his overture to Motorola in January 2007 in the form of a voicemail to CEO Ed Zander, who was attending the annual conference in Davos, Switzerland, with his chief operating officer, Greg Brown, today head of Motorola Solutions. Zander was also on the board of Time Warner, where Icahn was agitating for change. Icahn might have been trying to line up help behind the scenes at Time Warner—or he might have been calling to say, "Hello, Moto." Brown told Zander, "You sure as hell have to talk to him." Zander called him back. It was "Hello, Moto."

Icahn took a 5 percent position in the company. His primary motivation: Motorola's excess cash. Zander had recently appeared on CNBC, and the interviewer asked him what he was going to do with the money. His reply, says Brown: "Probably put it on the ground and roll around in it." Motorola was also having operational troubles. Its signature product, the Razr cell phone, was popular but getting less so; its price was falling, too. And the mobile phone division, the biggest in the company, was in bad shape and had the potential to crater the whole Motorola conglomerate.

Brown says, "What people saw was Maria Sharapova and David Beckham selling the Razr in a bunch of different colors. But we had

dozens of other phones, and five operating systems, multiple semicon-
ductors, three different software stacks. We were a marketing cam-
paign. A very good one. But it masked a terribly managed company."

Icahn put two representatives on the Motorola board. Icahn's advice,
says Brown, was "break the company up, break the company up, break
the company up." Zander resisted. He thought the cell phone, a business Motorola pioneered, was still the company's future. Eventually
Zander was forced out. Brown replaced him, and Icahn telephoned
him shortly thereafter. As Brown recalls, "Basically he said, 'This company has been mismanaged for years. I don't know who you are, but
you're the guy who has to fix it. You've got six to nine months to move
the needle or we'll get somebody else in there.'"

Brown's reaction is an excellent guide for how to deal with an activist while protecting long-term value. He concluded that he should not
resist Icahn's advice about what to do just because he was an outsider.
"I wasn't hung up with Icahn or the optics of it. If it's a good idea re-
gardless of the source, let's entertain it," he says. "The natural reaction
when Icahn enters the company is for the antibodies to come up. But I
said, 'Look, if he can be a catalyst for change, why wouldn't I do it?'"

Within months, Brown fired the head of the cell phone business,
went to Wall Street and lowered earnings expectations dramatically,
and announced plans to spin out the mobile division. Brown says, "I
thought it was a tremendous opportunity for management to drive
change because we had a massively sick business and we had a vocal,
massively muscular activist demanding change. There's not one change
Icahn pushed that I disagreed with."

Except for one—to sell the remaining Motorola entity, which was
focused primarily on public safety and emergency communications, as
soon as they spun out the mobile division. It would become their only
point of disagreement. It had taken three years to break up the company. Brown was not about to put a for-sale sign on the lawn. Icahn
responded that Brown couldn't be sure he would be able to lift the
share price of the company and was just trying to protect his position.
Brown pointed out all the moves he had already made at Icahn's urg-

ing, including selling off the bulk of the company. He said, "I've shown I'm willing to make changes. Let me run it, and if a buyer comes along, fine. But let me improve operations."

The board backed Brown. Icahn eventually sold his 23.7 million shares of Motorola Solutions for $49.15 a share. In early 2020, the stock hit a high of $187. "I should have never sold," he later told Brown. "You screwed me over on that deal." He was really only joking; it had been his decision to sell. And he still made over $500 million in profits on his Motorola investments.

Standing up to Icahn showed the investor that Brown was ready to take charge. But what really made their relationship was Brown's decision to accept a change that diluted his managerial control. After Brown fired the head of the mobility division, he sought a replacement with technical expertise to lead the business until Motorola was able to spin it off. Brown found a candidate who agreed to take the job—Qualcomm COO Sanjay Jha. But at the last minute, Brown got word that Jha wouldn't come unless he became co-CEO of the entire company. Brown thought Jha was bluffing; he would be CEO of the mobile business anyway as soon as it was spun off. Brown's instinct was to call the bluff. The board said it would back him whatever he wanted to do.

Brown got a phone call from Keith Meister, one of Icahn's representatives on the Motorola board. Meister asked him what he planned. Brown said that he would think about it, but he didn't think he wanted to give Jha the co-CEO position, especially after the way Jha had gone about demanding it. Meister told Brown, "Icahn is going to be paying close attention to this decision. Don't screw it up."

There was no question in Brown's mind that Jha was the right person for the job. And he thought there was a 90 percent chance that Jha would take the job even if he didn't get what he was asking for. Brown talked it over with someone he often turns to when he needs a sounding board—his son Troy—who told him that it was a no-brainer: if there were a one in ten chance of losing Jha, he'd be crazy to take that risk. On Monday, Brown agreed to give Jha the co-CEO title. His take: "To this day Carl Icahn says that it's the single best decision

I made, and it cemented his opinion of me. He tells me, 'Most people think of their ego and cover their ass, and you made the decision that was right for Motorola and wrong for you.' That made my reputation with him."

The relationship with Icahn left Brown with a different impression of activists. Brown describes Icahn as "a combination of Walter Matthau, Columbo, and Professor John Nash from *A Beautiful Mind*, with a mean streak." He can be intimidating and in your face, but Brown finds his bluntness and directness refreshing. Brown says, "The beautiful thing about Carl is whatever he's going to do to the company or the board, he's going to tell me. Carl comes right at you, in large part to test your fortitude and your own conviction."

Icahn would often ask Brown the same question over and over again. It dawned on Brown that Icahn knew the answer and just wanted to see if Brown's answer was the same each time. If there was any deviation, Icahn wanted to know why. In the beginning, Brown feared that constant pounding, but over time, it freed him to be more honest himself. He says, "I could communicate with Icahn. I could say anything. I went from fear to a more comfortable engagement." Though Icahn exited the company after six years, the two stay in touch and have dinner two or three times a year.

Brown now believes that the goals of most activists are not that different from those of regular investors. He says, "Largely, the activist shareholder and the generalist shareholder have more in common than they don't. When you say these activists are more short term and hit-and-run, that can be grounded in management's convenient narrative not to do what activists are suggesting you should."

Activists break down business issues into a set of facts and numbers with very clear assumptions. It's up to you to conclude which is right or wrong. Often the management narrative is not converted to shareholder value, so it becomes a debate over the same thing, a difference in style more than substance. Icahn was the right activist for Motorola, and for Brown, at the right time.

Brown learned that the main trick in dealing with an activist investor is knowing when to sacrifice your ego and say yes and knowing when to say no. The aim: always to make the changes that build the long-term value of the company—whether the idea is yours or not.

CHECKLIST FOR ENGAGING WITH INVESTORS

- Reach out to some of your investors every year. Invite them in to make presentations.

- Find out what investors know about you, their sources, and the metrics they use to rate you against your competitors.

- Prepare to tell investors how you ensure that management is focused on long-term value creation.

- Prepare to tell investors about succession procedures and the rationale for executive salary, bonuses, performance rewards, and other compensation.

- Say yes to any investor who requests a meeting.

- Connect with investors after earnings calls.

- Don't let your company give earnings guidance. If it's absolutely necessary, express it in a wide range.

- Stay close to your big institutional investors; without their support, no activist can force their way onto your board.

- Don't rule out inviting an activist onto your board if they show an interest in creating long-term value.

- Keep an open mind if an investor suggests a change. Go by the logic, not the optics of agreeing to it.

ESG

The Big Picture, Not Just a Piece of the Puzzle

Our aim in writing this book was to help directors redefine the concept of total shareholder return by taking the long view and focusing on the key considerations of talent, strategy, and risk.

In the interviews we conducted with dozens of company leaders and directors, the subject of environmental, social, and governance (ESG) issues came up quite frequently. And from our own experience in working with boards, we know that ESG is top of mind for many directors. You may have noticed, however, that we did not include a separate chapter on ESG or address it as a stand-alone topic. Why not? Because ESG is not a separate topic, and ESG-related themes are woven throughout the book. In a sense, you can't spell TSR without ESG.

When we talked about talent in this book, we discussed human capital management, diversity, and healthy corporate cultures. When we talked about strategy, we discussed the sustainability of business models and the ability to anticipate shifts in consumer demand. When we talked about risk, we discussed the things that can go wrong: banking scandals, airline disasters, pandemics, sexual harassment, social and economic injustice, the worsening climate crisis. These are all ESG conversations.

Ultimately, all of these matters fall under the purview of the directors who are elected to govern a company—the G in ESG. Boards must own and understand how their companies can affect or be affected by these factors.

Telling Your Story

How should companies report on ESG? There is no shortage of options or opinions. In recent years, we've witnessed an explosion in the number of market-based reporting frameworks, while regulatory reporting requirements continue to evolve around the world at an uneven pace. It has been a point of frustration for companies and investors alike. The common refrain we've heard from boards and management teams has been, "Just tell us which framework to use." At the same time, investors have been calling for information that is clear, consistent, and comparable to enable better decisions.

We've been encouraged by ongoing efforts to drive standardization of ESG reporting practices—particularly through the work of groups such as the Sustainability Accounting Standards Board and the Task Force on Climate-related Financial Disclosures. This movement calls to mind the efforts to standardize accounting standards and principles nearly a century ago. Whether ESG reporting standards come into being through market-based initiatives, regulation, or a combination of the two, these standards are necessary for the benefit of operating companies and investors alike.

For investors, context can be just as important as raw data. Every company has its own ESG story, strategy, and unique set of challenges. Companies need to recognize the areas where they may be viewed as an outlier and ask: Are we a leader, are we a laggard, and how do we tell that story so that investors will understand?

In the Long Run, a Convergence of Interests

In the introduction, we talked about the Business Roundtable's call for companies to serve more than their shareholders. Its 2019 Statement on the Purpose of a Corporation said that companies should also provide value to stakeholders such as customers, employees, communities, and suppliers. The statement caused quite a bit of confusion and debate, especially in boardrooms and among those charged with overseeing fiduciary duties to shareholders. Some people were worried that it signified a complete upending of the system, and that it relegated shareholders to being just another stakeholder. Those concerns have been unfounded, and we're not seeing a rewriting of market expectations in this regard.

Shareholders provide capital to companies to generate returns. That's the reason people invest, as survey after survey has confirmed. For all of the chaos, risk, and uncertainty that are inherent in the capital markets, the market also values order. When there is no structure or clarity of expectations for a company among its shareholders and stakeholders, then management and the board essentially become accountable for nothing. And when company leaders are not accountable, things fall apart.

We believe the consensus view of the Business Roundtable statement is that it's a pragmatic recognition of the way companies are evolving. More and more companies understand that shareholder value is not created in a vacuum. If a company operates without care or concern for its customers, employees, suppliers, or communities, it will destroy shareholder value over the long run. Indeed, over the long run, the interests of shareholders and stakeholders converge.

Shelly Lazarus put this nicely in chapter 2 when she described the ongoing shift toward business sustainability. "It's now part of how the best companies are run because it's becoming increasingly important to all the constituents of any company," she said. "If you're market driven, the market has spoken about whether these things are important or not—how you treat your resources, how you interact with the community, how long term you are in your thinking about your impact on society."

For instance, one focus of ESG is curbing waste. No company can improve air quality on its own, but any company can make a unilateral decision to stop polluting. It may need to change its business model and invest in new manufacturing and product development technologies, but in the long run, reducing waste will cut costs, boost profits, and create long-term value.

Educational initiatives can work in the same way. Many US companies have invested in education, either directly or through foundations. Far from being an act of charity, the aim is to help make sure that the employees of tomorrow have the skills companies will need. Such programs can also help redress the financial inequality that is threatening to tear this country apart. Public companies have a role to play in this realm. And a growing number of investors, especially younger ones, will expect companies to take that role seriously.

In the end, the essence of the debate is not shareholder versus stakeholder, but short term versus long term. For more than a decade, investors like Vanguard have been promoting the development of a longer view, one recognizing that long-term value creation is really what most investors are interested in.

Leading an organization for the long term is easy in theory. But the long term is made up of thousands of short terms, and it can be nearly impossible for a company to meet the interests of all of its constituents all of the time. The pressure to satisfy shareholders and stakeholders can be intense. Earlier in the book, Jeffrey Ubben said, "Sustainability is a solve for short-termism." Well stated—though it takes courage and vision, and will lead to an organization that is focused on long-term sustainability.

That's why boards are critical. A board is the steward of long-term value for a company's shareholders and stakeholders. At any given time, the sitting members of a board can span several decades of service. That's longer than most CEOs will serve and longer than many investors will hold the stock. As a perpetual governing body, the board has the unique perspective and ability to oversee, counsel, and ultimately empower the company to create sustainable long-term value.

INDEX

AbbVie, 41, 74, 85, 86
accountability, 82, 96
  CEO, 104–105
  compensation committee and,
    123–124
Ackman, William, 160
activists
  alpha, 167–171
  balance sheet, 140
  on the board, 160–162
  destructive, 162–163
  how to deal with, 157–163
  influence of, xi
  information on perspective of,
    139–144
  meeting with, 150
  moves by, 159–160
  P&L, 140
  pressure from, boards and, 7
  risks from, 71
  sustainability and, 65–66
  thinking like, 164–167
  types of, 158–159
adaptable organizations, 46, 49–51, 78
Adelphia, xii
ad hoc committees, 130–131
Adobe, 50–51
AECOM, 72
AI, 47
Allen, Herb, 26, 98
Amazon, 6, 18
  joint ventures with, 53
  moneymaking model of, 48

American Express, 105
Arthur, W. Brian, 47–48
assessment
  of boards, 19, 96, 107–110
  of CEO candidates, 21–23
  of CEO performance, 28–29
  of committee chairs, 120
  450-degree, 31
  leadership development and,
    30–31
  of leadership teams, 35–36
  of performance, 122, 141–143, 145
  of strategy performance, 61–63
assumptions, in CEO selection, 21
audit committee, 76–77, 126–127
  at Berkshire Hathaway, 87–88
  role of, 118–119
audits
  culture, 19, 41, 122–123
  governance, 87–88
  human capital, 19, 74–75
auto industry, 32

bad actors, 71, 84–88
Ballmer, Steve, 161
Bank of America, 53
Barra, Mary, 8, 11. *See also* General
  Motors
  board communication with, 49
  on board information, 137–138
  on board refreshment, 113
  on culture, 43–44

Barra, Mary (*continued*)
  on cybersecurity, 83
  market modeling and, 51–52
  on openness with investors, 155
  talent management by, 18–19, 32
Barton, Dominic, 30
Beneficial Bank, 61
Berkshire Hathaway, 8, 10, 102–103
  audit committee at, 87–88
  mergers and acquisitions at, 57
Bernstein Research, xiii
Bezos, Jeff, 6, 18
biopharma, 59–60
BlackRock, 1, 64, 153, 165
Blockbuster, 46, 49
boards of directors, xi, xv
  activists on, 160–162
  benchmarking, 93
  best practices for, 92–94
  capabilities for, 10–11
  CEO oversight and, 17, 28–29
  CEO responsibilities *vs.*, 128–129
  CEO selection and, 17, 20–23
  checklist for creating capable,
    115–116
  committee redesign for, 11, 93,
    117–131
  communication between meetings
    by, 81–82
  compensation committee, 11
  compensation of, 113–115
  composition of, 19
  customer interaction with, 54–55
  diversity in, 100–101
  employee interaction with, 34–35
  engagement of with investors, 2,
    11–12, 93, 147–171
  evaluation of, 19, 96, 107–110
  execution committee, 11
  executive sessions, 105–107
  expectations for, 113

  expertise and skills for, 72–73, 93,
    95–116
  goal setting for, 108–109
  in governance *vs.* management, 63
  importance of, 177
  industry insiders and outsiders on,
    98
  information diversification for, 11,
    93, 133–146
  information seeking by, 144–145
  leadership in, 104–105
  leadership team development and,
    29–36
  leading for tomorrow by, 6–8
  market modeling and, 51–53
  meeting frequency for, 8
  meetings with investors, 149–157
  the new TSR focus for, 3–5,
    15–16
  redefining for the long term, 1–12
  refreshing, 111–113
  the right setting for, 105–107
  risk appetite of, 70, 77–78
  risk prioritization by, 70–72
  selection criteria for, 97, 101–104
  size of, 100
  succession planning and, 24–27
  technology committee, 11
  time constraints on, 117–118
  travel by, 127
Boeing, 29, 41, 86, 102
Bogle, Jack, ix
Booz Allen Hamilton, 83
Botelho, Elena, 21, 49, 78, 104
  on goal setting, 108–109
Breen, Ed, 35, 137, 162
Brennan, Jack, ix
  on activists on the board, 162–163
  on board continuity and change,
    111
  on curated information, 138–139

on dealing with activists, 158

on governance, xii

on governance *vs.* management, 63

on investment structure, 166

on risk management, 84

on talent management, 33

Broussard, Bruce, 21

Brown, Greg, 167–171

Buckley, Tim, 33

Buffett, Warren, 8, 9

on activist perspective, 139–140

on bad actors, 87–88

on bad behavior, 85

on board compensation, 114

on board diversity, 101

on board members as pawns, 102–103

on CEO compensation, 36–37

at Coca-Cola, 108

on information for boards, 139

on mergers and acquisitions, 57, 60

on openness with investors, 155–156

on risk, 10

on settings for boards, 106

on strategy evaluation, 61–62

test for auditors, 71, 87

Burnison, Gary, 72

business models, 47

Business Roundtable, 1, 7–8, 175

Calhoun, David, 29

CamberView Partners, 104–105

capitalism, stakeholder *vs.* shareholder, 65–66

capital markets, importance of, xiii–xiv

cash generation, 48

Catalent, 75–76, 110

CA Technologies, 141–143

CEOs

board committees and, 117–118

board communication with, 135

board information and, 137–138, 144–145

as board members, 103–104

board responsibilities and, 128–129

compensation for, 3, 36–37

culture and, 42, 43–44

disruptive technologies and, 52–53

executive sessions and, 107

field-testing, 22–23

on goal setting, 108–109

internal candidate vetting for, 21–22

leadership team development and, 29–36

leadership team turnover and, 41–42

lead independent directors and, 104–105

long-term focus by, 6

in meetings with investors, 154–156

oversight of, 17, 28–29

selection of, 17, 20–23

simulations in testing, 21

strategy and risk committee and, 124–125

succession planning and, 19, 24–27

CFOs, 137

change of control provisions, 75

checklists

for board capabilities, 115–116

for engaging with investors, 171

for information diversification, 146

for redesigning committees, 131

for risk management, 88–89

for strategy management, 68

for talent management, 44

chief human resources officers, 39–40

Chiminski, John, 75–76
Christianson, Wei, 100
Citigroup, 76
Citrix, 165
climate change, 1, 64–67
coaching and mentoring, 28, 35–36
Coca-Cola, 25–27, 98, 108
codes of conduct, 86
committees, 11, 93, 117–131
    ad hoc and temporary, 130–131
    audit, 76–77, 87–88, 126–127
    chairs of, 120
    checklist for redesigning, 131
    compensation, 11, 19
    cybersecurity, 129–130
    evaluation of, 120
    execution, 11, 19
    independence of, 119
    information independence and 96,
        128, 134 (*see also* information)
    nominating and governance,
        127–129
    organizing, 118–120
    strategy and risk, 76–77, 82,
        124–126
    talent, compensation, and execu-
        tion, 120–124
    technology, 11, 99
communication, xiii
    about CEOs under fire, 29
    between board meetings, 81–82
    with committees, 120
    moneymaking model and, 48–49
    pacing of, 153
    skills in, 102
    on strategy, 53–54
compensation, 36–37, 121–122
    of boards, 113–115
    CEO, 3, 36–37
    of committee chairs, 120
    culture and, 41

investor interest in, 152
    tied to short-term results, 3
compensation committee, 11. *See also*
    talent, compensation, and exe-
    cution committee
    talent development and, 19
competitive advantage, 51
competitive threats, 47
confirmation bias, 56
consultants, 37, 112, 122
Cook Pharmica, 75–76
Countrywide Financial, 53
Covid-19 pandemic, xv, 67
credibility
    building, 166
    loss of, 29
Cruise, 37, 52
culture
    audits of, 19, 41, 122–123
    bad behavior and, 85–88
    talent and, 41–44
customers, 46
    strategy and, 54–55
cybersecurity committee, 129–130
cybersecurity risk, 71, 82–85,
    98–99

Danaher Corp., 58–60
dashboards, 48–49, 84
data analytics, 46
Data Documents, 140
data gap, 135
deal assassins, 56–57
debt strategies, 72
decision making, 42–43, 45–46
    strategy and, 55
Dell Computer, 6
Delphi Automotive, 8, 53–54, 57.
    See also Gupta, Rajiv
    risk matrix for, 80–81

Delphi Systems, 9
digital technologies, 47
    activists and, 165–166
    board expertise in, 98–99
    increasing returns and, 47–48
Diller, Barry, 98
Directors' Council, 8, 11, 29. *See also*
        Hooper, Michele
    strategy at, 55
    strategy evaluation at, 62
disruptive technologies, 52–53,
        77–78
diversity, 1, 19
    on boards, 100–101
    strategy and risk committee and,
        125–126
    talent pool, 38–40
divestment, 57–58
division of labor, in boards, 11
Dow, 162
Drexel Directors Dialogue, xii, 2
DuPont, 12, 161–162

economic crises, 1
educational initiatives, 176
Eli Lilly, 144
E.L. Rothschild, 145
employee retention, 145
Enron, xii, 41, 86
enterprise risk management (ERM),
        79–80
environmental, social, and gover-
        nance (ESG) issues, 173–177
Erdoes, Mary, 39, 60
    on audit committees, 127
    on courage in board members, 102
    in investor conferences, 166–167
Estée Lauder, 72–73, 100, 150
ethical behavior, 84–88. *See also* so-
        cial responsibility

execution, 47, 122–124
    moneymaking models and, 48–49,
        55
execution committee, 11. *See also*
        talent, compensation, and exe-
        cution committee
    talent development and, 19
executive committee, 130
executive sessions, 105–107

Facebook, 53
Fanandakis, Nick, 161–162
Federal Reserve, 75
feedback
    board evaluation and, 107–110
    to CEOs, 29
    on risk, 81
    to/from investors, 153–154
Ferguson, Roger, 28, 73
Fields, Mark, 25
    on activists as board members, 163
field-testing, 21–23
field visits, 34
financial services, trends in, 52, 61
Fink, Larry, 64, 165
Ford, William, 24, 25
Ford Motor Co., 72–73, 163
    succession planning at, 24–25
    talent development at, 18
Forester de Rothschild, Lady Lynn,
        100, 145, 150
Friedman, Abe, 104–105
Friedman, Milton, 8

Garden, Ed, 30, 42
    on activists, 159
    on CEO experience for board
        members, 103
    on compensation committee, 123

Garden, Ed (*continued*)
  on information asymmetry, 135
  on Wendy's, 130, 143
Garnier, Jean-Pierre, 22
GE, 11, 141–143
  leadership development at, 31–32
  talent development at, 18
GE Capital, 142
General Motors (GM), 8, 9, 11. *See
    also* Barra, Mary
  compensation at, 37
  diversity at, 40
  job rotation at, 33–34
  market modeling at, 51–52
  meetings with investors at, 154–155
  strategy information at, 49
  talent management at, 18–19, 32
  technology risk at, 83–84
geopolitical risk, 70–71
ghSMART, 21, 49, 78, 104
globalization, 70–71
GM. *See* General Motors (GM)
goals, 108–109, 126
Goizueta, Roberto, 25
Gooden, Linda, 113
Google, 31, 86
governance, xi
  audits of, 87–88
  committees, 127–129
  failures in, xii
  management *vs.*, 63
  redefining for the long term, 1–12
Griesedieck, Joseph, 104
GSK, 22
Gupta, Rajiv, 8, 53–54
  activist perspective and, 139
  on board communication, 81–82
  on meeting with investors, 150
  on portfolio management, 57
  on replacing board members,
    112–113
  risk matrix by, 80–81

H1N1 swine flu, 10, 79–80
Hackett, Jim, 25
Hockaday, Irv, 24, 72–73
Hooper, Michele, 8, 11
  on board evaluation, 110
  on board skills, 99
  on CEO selection, 29
  information acquisition by, 145
  on skills development, 140–141
  on strategy, 55
  on strategy evaluation, 62
  town halls by, 34–35
HR. *See* human resources (HR)
Humana, 21
human capital audits, 19, 74–75
human resources (HR), 55
  boardroom representation of, 19
hybrid strategy, 47

IBM, talent development at, 18
Icahn, Carl, 167–170
Immelt, Jeffrey, 142
inclusion, 19
Inclusive Capital Partners, 65–66,
    100, 145
index funds, ix, xii
  investor influence and, 148
  the new TSR and, 3–4
information
  activist perspective in, 139–144
  from activists, 158–160
  asymmetry in, 11
  checklist for diversifying, 146
  curated *vs.* overloaded, 138–139
  diversification of board, 11, 47, 93,
    133–146
  independence of, 134
  making sense of, 141–143
  from management, 136–139
  meeting with investors for,
    149–157

from outsiders, 140–141
sharing of for boards, 105–107
strategic initiatives and, 61
on talent, 18, 20, 34
initiatives for value creation
  compensation linked to, 37
  dashboards for, 48–49
  educational, 176
  evaluating, 3
  strategic, 60–61
  sustainability, 66
institutional investors
  board relationships with, 7
  on short-termism, 5
intellectual property theft, 85
investment patterns, 48, 73–75, 166
investors. *See also* activists
  board engagement with, 2, 11–12,
    93, 147–171
  changes in, ix–xv
  checklist for engaging with, 171
  cost of failure for, 148
  as drivers of the new TSR,
    147–148
  giving guidance to, 156–157
  meeting with, 149–157
  needs of long-term, ix–xiii
  the new TSR and, 3–4
  sustainability and, 64
  telling your story to, 174–175
  what they want to know, 151–153

Jacobs Manufacturing Co., 58–60
Jha, Sanay, 169–170
Johnson & Johnson, 40–41
joint ventures, 47, 53
Joyce, Tom, 59
J.P. Morgan Asset & Wealth Man-
    agement, 20, 39. *See also* Erdoes,
    Mary
  audit committee at, 127

on guidance to investors, 156
investor conference at, 166–167
joint ventures with, 53
strategic initiatives at, 60

Kent, Muhtar, 26–27
key performance indicators, 128–129
knowledge-based industries, 47–48
Kodak, 46
Korn Ferry, 2, 31, 72
Kozlowski, Dennis, 79–80

Lauder, William, 100
Lazarus, Shelly, 40, 64–65, 82–83,
    143–144
  on activists on the board, 163
  on investor information, 153
  on sustainability, 175–176
leaders and leadership, 15
  board refreshment and, 111–112
  for boards, 93
  on boards, 104–105, 127–128
  board selection and oversight of,
    17, 20–23, 28–29, 35–36
  CEO field-testing and, 23
  comfort zones of, 53
  continuity of, crises and, 73–74
  development of at Coca-Cola,
    25–27
  evaluation of, 108–109, 110
  information independence and,
    134
  long-term strategy and, 53–58
  outside intelligence on, 35
  risk from bad behavior by, 71,
    84–88
  selection criteria for, 97
  skills/talents for the future and,
    30–31
  succession planning for, xv

leaders and leadership (*continued*)
  team creation, 29–36
  testing, 26–27
  turnover in, culture problems and, 41–42
  women in, 39–40
lead independent director (LID), 104–105
  committee structure and, 119–120
  compensation committee and, 124
Levenson, Rodger, 23
LID. *See* lead independent director (LID)
liquidity, 72–73, 75–78
  activists and, 158–159, 165
long-term value creation, 5
  board capabilities for, 10–11
  boards as drivers in, 164
  CEOs and, 20
  collaboration between boards and CEOs and, 117
  disruption and, 78
  at Inclusive Capital Partners, 66
  investors and, 149–157
  managing risk and, 78, 81
  the new TSR for, 8–12
  specialists and, 100
  stakeholders and, 65
  sustainability and, 64–66
  talent and, 17, 43, 73
  at Wendy's, 143
Lowe's, 80
LSC Communications, 72
Lucent, 85

macroeconomic risk, 70–71
management, governance *vs.*, 63
margins, expanding, 58–60
market modeling, 51–53
Martin, Aaron, 125–126

McCracken, Bill, 141–143
McGinn, Rich, 85
McKinsey, 31
Merck, 82–83
mergers and acquisitions, 9, 47, 52–53
  activist interest in, 157–158
  opposing points of view on, 56–57
  strategically correct, 58–60
  strategic risk and, 75–76
  strategy and, 55
  talent risk and, 74–75
Merrill Lynch, 53
#MeToo, 41
metrics, 48–49, 152–153
Microsoft, 18, 46, 159, 161
moneymaking models, 46, 47–51
  bad actors and, 85
  board expertise on, 99
  market modeling and, 51–53
  strategy and, 55
Motorola, 167–170
Muilenberg, Dennis, 29
Mulally, Alan, 24–25
Mulcahy, Anne, 40–41, 153
  on activists, 160
  on board continuity and change, 111
  on social responsibility, 64
Musk, Elon, 163
mutual fund assets, ix

Narayen, Shantanu, 50–51
Nasser, Jacques, 24
Netflix, 49
net promoter scores, 141
new TSR
  board composition and, 95–96
  committee structure and, 117–118
  and decision-making, 45–46
  definition, 3–5

execution and, 48
index funds and, 3–4
investors as drivers of, 147–148
for long-term value creation,
    8–12
and risk, 69–70
at Vanguard, 5
Nokia, 161
nominating and governance com-
    mittee, 127–129
Nooyi, Indra, 6
NotPetya, 82–83

Ogilvy & Mather, 64, 143, 153
O'Hanley, Ron, 62, 80
    on activists as board members,
        163
    on board committees, 118
    on board knowledge, 98
    on outside perspectives, 144
operating committee, 130
operations, culture and, 42–43

pacing, of communication, 153
Pall, 59–60
pandemics, 72–73
    Covid-19, xv, 67
    H1N1, 10, 79–80
Paris Agreement, 67
Peltz, Nelson, 161–162
PepsiCo, 6, 110
performance analytics, 31, 122,
    141–143, 145
performance evaluation, 122, 141–
    143, 145
    activists and, 164–166
    for investors, 151
    of strategy, 61–63
Pershing Square, 160
Pfizer, 144

Phillips 66, 119–120
Pitney Bowes, 34
Plexiglas, 58
Pozen, Daniel, 154
PPG, 29
premerger bakeoffs, 57
proactive mindset, 39
promotions, 43
Providence Health, 11, 125–126
public corporations, 77
    board inefficacy and, 6–7
public good, 63–64

Qualcomm, 169
Quincey, James, 25–27

racial inequity, 1
Rales, Mitchell, 58–60
Rales, Steven, 58–60
Ratnakar, Raj, 59, 60
recruitment, 38–39, 101
regulation, 7, 18, 174
Relational Investors, 150
Reliance Steel & Aluminum, 72
reporting, 174–175
reputation risk, 84
resiliency, 128–129
resource allocation, 45, 72–73
retirement age, mandatory, 111
Richmond, Tim, 41, 74, 86
Riff, Dan, 66, 151
risk, 3–5, 9–10, 15, 69–89. *See also*
    strategy and risk committee
    acceptance of, 73
    ad hoc committees and, 130
    audit committee and, 126–127
    of bad behavior, 71, 84–88
    centralization of, 82–83
    checklist for managing, 88–89
    cybersecurity, 82–84

risk (*continued*)
  diversification of information and, 134
  immediate, 70–72
  investor interest in, 152
  liquidity and, 158–159
  matrix of, 80–81
  resources for surviving, 72–73
  strategic, 75–78
  talent-related, 73–75
  total enterprise, 78–84
  types of, 69–72
Robinson, Jim III, 105
Rockwell Collins, 56–57
Rogers, Brian, 56–57, 80
  on bad actors, 84
  on digital expertise, 98–99
  on giving guidance to investors, 156
  on guidance to investors, 156
Rohm & Haas, 58

Sarbanes-Oxley Act of 2002, xii
Sears, 165
Seidenberg, Ivan, 34, 111–112
shareholders, 63. *See also* investors
  primacy of, 1
  stakeholders *vs.*, xiv
  total shareholder return and, 2–3
  value redefinition, 7
short-termism, 3–5
simulations, 21
skill development, 31–32. *See also* talent
  activist perspective and, 140–141
  for employees, 176
  workforce preparation, 140–141, 176
social responsibility, 7–8
  environmental, social, and governance issues and, 173–177

investor interest in, 152
  strategy, stakeholders, and, 63–67
  talent retention and, 40–41
Spencer Stuart, 38
stakeholders, 118
  balancing interests of, 8
  boards and, 93, 94
  long-term value creation and, 65
  shareholders and, 175–177
  shareholders *vs.*, xiv
  strategy for all, 63–67
  value for, 175
Statement on the Purpose of a Corporation, 175
State Street, 62, 80. *See also* O'Hanley, Ron
Stotlar, Doug, 72
strategy, 3–5, 9, 15, 45–68
  activists' perspective on, 144
  adaptability and, 46, 49–51
  for all stakeholders, 63–67
  CEO succession linked to, 21
  checklist for managing, 68
  communication about, 53–54
  diversification of information and, 133
  failures in, 55–56
  initiatives and, 60–61
  investor days and, 166–167
  investor interest in, 152
  for the long term, 53–58
  market modeling and, 51–53
  moneymaking models and, 46, 47–51, 55
  monitoring, 45–46, 48
  performance evaluation of, 61–63
  risk related to, 75–78
  talent and, 45, 53–54
strategy and risk committee, 76–77, 82, 118, 124–126

subscription models, 50–51
succession planning, xv, 19
  for boards, 127–128
  emergency, 73–74
  at GM, 19
  investor interest in, 152
  judgment calls in, 24–27
  talent, compensation, and execu-
    tion committee in, 121
  talent development and, 20, 21
supply-chain risk, 72
sustainability, 1, 64–67, 173–177
  measuring, 66
  reporting on, 174–175
  strategy and, 63–67
  talent retention and, 40–41
Sustainability Accounting Standards
  Board, 174
Swords, Brendan, 102

talent, 3–5, 17–44, 173–174. *See also*
  leaders and leadership
  for boards, 10–11, 93, 95–116
  changing employee base and,
    32–33
  checklist for managing, 44
  competition for, 18
  culture and, 41–44
  diversification of information on,
    133
  diversity in, 38–40
  engagement of, 37–38
  importance of, 9, 17
  investor interest in, 152
  management and oversight of,
    18–19
  retaining, 36–41, 73
  risk related to, 73–75
  strategy and, 45, 47, 53–54
  sustainability and, 64
  trends in, 32

talent, compensation, and execution
  committee, 118, 120–124
  meetings with investors, 154–156
talent development
  boards in, 20–21
  culture and, 43
  job rotation and, 33–34
  for leadership teams, 29–36
Talent Wins (Charan, Carey & Barton), 30
Target, 160
Task Force on Climate-related
  Financial Disclosures, 174
technology committee, 11, 99,
  129–130
technology risk, 82–83. *See also*
  cybersecurity risk
Tesla, 163
test for auditors, Buffett's, 71, 87
Thornton, John, 24–25, 73
Thunberg, Greta, 67
TIAA, 28, 73
time constraints, 117
Time Warner, 167
total shareholder return (TSR), 2–3,
  173
Toyota, 58–60
training, strategy and, 53–54
transparency, 105–106
  in meetings with investors,
    154–156
Trans World Airlines, 167
travel, 127
Trian Partners, 30, 142. *See also*
  Garden, Ed
  Wendy's and, 143
T. Rowe Price, 80, 84, 98–99, 156,
  158
Tsay, Caroline, 98
TSR. *See* risk; strategy; talent; total
  shareholder return (TSR)
TSR, new. *See* new TSR

Turner, Mark
  on customer focus, 54
  field-testing by, 22–23
  on leadership selection, 20, 32
  market modeling and, 52
  on risk management, 81
  on strategic risk, 77
  on talent engagement, 37–38
Tyco International, 10, 35, 79–80,
    86, 137
  activists at, 150

Ubben, Jeffrey, 65–66, 77
  on activists, 159
  boards and risk, 77
  at Microsoft, 161
  on strategy and risk committee,
    124–125
  on sustainability, 176
undervalued stock, 166
Unilever, 40
UnitedHealth Group, 34–35, 99,
    140–141
United Technologies, 56–57, 80

ValueAct Capital, 65–66, 161
value creation, 74
  boards in long-term, 6–8
  public good vs., 63–64
  short- and long-term, 48–49
Vanguard, ix–x, xiii
  diversity at, 38–39
  meetings with investors at, 150
  the new TSR at, 5
  operating committee at, 130
  shareholder focus at, xi–xii

talent development at, 33
  three Cs at, xiv
  voice of long-term investors at,
    xi–xiii
Vanguard 500 Index Fund, ix
Verizon, 34, 111–112
vision, 101–102
Volkswagen, 41, 86

Walmart, 18, 165
Weismann, Bob, 34
Wellington Capital Group, 158
Wellington Management, 102, 154
Wells Fargo, 41, 62, 86
Wendy's, 11, 129–130, 143
WhatsApp, 53
Williams, Ron, 73–74
Witty, Andrew, 22
women, 39–40, 101. *See also*
    diversity
workforce preparation, 140–141, 176
World Bank, xiii
WorldCom, xii
worst-case scenarios, 72–73
WSFS Financial Corp., 9, 20
  CEO field-testing at, 22–23
  customer focus at, 54
  market modeling and, 52
  risk management at, 81
  talent refreshment at, 37–38

Xerox, 64, 153

Zander, Ed, 167–171

ACKNOWLEDGMENTS

We are deeply grateful to the many CEOs, directors, and C-suite executives who gave us interview time and contributed mightily to sharpening our view of how to convert big ideas into the easily executable actions presented in this book. Our many investor contributors, including Warren Buffett, also provided extraordinary support in backing our thesis that it's all about getting three things right—talent, strategy, and risk—to advance enterprise value, the right kind of growth, and long-term potential for all who put their money in the market.

Our special thanks go to Herb Allen, Mary Barra, Elena Botelho, Ed Breen, Jack Brennan, Bruce Broussard, Mary Erdoes, Lady Lynn Forester de Rothschild, Abe Friedman, Ed Garden, Raj Gupta, Michele Hooper, Muhtar Kent, Shelly Lazarus, Bill McCracken, Anne Mulcahy, Sam Nunn, Ron O'Hanley, Dan Riff, Brian Rogers, Kevin Sneader, Brendan Swords, Mark Turner, and Jeff Ubben. Thanks also for comments from Kenneth Abrams, John Averill, Eunhak Bae, Nicolas Choumenkovitch, Wendy Cromwell, Bob Hallagan, Evan Hornbuckle, Tom Levering, Gregory Mattiko, Dave Palmer, Dan Pozen, Saul Rubin, Tara Stilwell, and Mark Whitaker.

Two people played pivotal roles in turning our mountain of ideas into readable text. The first is our editor at Harvard Business Review Press, Melinda Merino. Using her grasp of trends and issues in business and its broader context, Melinda helped define what the book should contain and how best to present it. Her oversight was substantive, immensely helpful, and encouraging in every instance. We couldn't be more grateful for her guidance.

The second is Andrew Kupfer, who masterfully turned input from three authors and an enormous pile of content into an eminently readable book that is respectful of readers' time. We reaped the benefit of

Andrew's years of experience as a journalist and editor at *Fortune*. The clarity of his thinking and his superb writing and editing skills won our admiration and took a great burden off our shoulders.

Our thanks also to the production staff at HBR, led by Anne Starr, whose expertise and attention to detail are world class. Also, to graphic designer Scott Berinato, who creatively translated our ideas into visual shorthand.

From Bill McNabb: I'm incredibly grateful to my colleagues at Vanguard for all their support on this project, starting with Tim Buckley, Anne Robinson, and Chris McIsaac. Their critical thinking and encouragement have been invaluable. Much of the data in the book came from multiple sources across Vanguard. Mike Buek, Andy Clarke, Kasia Kraszweska, Ryan Ludt, Mike Nolan, Jim Rowley, Amanda Shah, and Haifeng Wang contributed greatly to this effort. Vanguard's governance experts—Glenn Booraem, Rob Wherry, and Sarah Relich—stood shoulder to shoulder with us; without them, this book would not have been possible. Last, "thank you" seems totally inadequate for Bryan Thomas and Vickie Leinhauser. They were involved in every aspect of this book and continue to be hugely supportive.

From Ram Charan: I'm lucky to have had many learning conversations and engagements with business leaders over the years, including Kumar Birla, Bob Bradway, Dick Brown, Chad Holliday, Lois Juliber, Jorge Paulo Lemann, Kathy Murphy, Doug Peterson, Helene Runtagh, Anna Saicali, Carlos Alberto Sicupira, Cecilia Sicupira, Sumant Sinha, Michael Useem, Ed Woolard, and Qin Yinglin. My longtime business partner, John Joyce, provided useful feedback and support throughout the writing process. My assistants Cynthia Burr and Lisa Laubert skillfully managed the logistical challenges and provided other essential support. Geri Willigan, who has worked with me on corporate governance issues since my first book on boards more than twenty years ago, was an essential contributor to this book as well.

From Dennis Carey: I want to thank Gary Burnison, the CEO I serve at Korn Ferry, who encourages everyone in the firm to advance new ideas, learn from those who run successful enterprises, and develop our profile in the right way in the markets we serve. Further, Donna Gregor, my assistant of thirty years, has been the key to my ability to get things done with care and confidence. I also want to thank Joe Griesedieck, vice chairman of Korn Ferry, who recruited me to this great firm. He has always been there to support my research projects, my client work, and other endeavors. He has been a friend and colleague for over thirty years, and I have learned from him the importance of bringing humor, decency, and diplomacy to everything we do. And a special note of thanks to my adopted family—Katrina, Moritz, Chamonix, Brighton, and Soleil—who made it fun for me to occasionally forget about work—and of course to my son Matt and daughter Maggie, who I have treasured quietly in my life's wonderful journey.

ABOUT THE AUTHORS

Bill McNabb is the former chairman and CEO of Vanguard, one of the world's largest investment management companies. He joined Vanguard in 1986 and became CEO in 2008 and chairman in 2010. He retired as CEO in 2017 and as chairman in 2018. During his tenure as chief executive, Vanguard's assets under management more than quadrupled to $4.4 trillion. McNabb has been an advocate for good corporate governance and responsible long-term investing through leadership roles with organizations such as Chief Executives for Corporate Purpose (CECP) and the Investment Company Institute. He also works with academic programs such as the Raj & Kamla Gupta Governance Institute at Drexel University's LeBow College of Business, the Ira M. Millstein Center for Global Markets and Corporate Ownership at Columbia Law School, and Wharton's Center for Leadership and Change Management. McNabb is a board member of UnitedHealth Group, IBM, Axiom, and Tilney Smith & Williamson. He is also chairman of Ernst & Young's Independent Audit Committee. He is passionate about education and serves as a board member of the Philadelphia School Partnership, as chairman of the board of the Philadelphia Zoo, and as a member of the Dartmouth Athletic Advisory Board. McNabb earned an AB at Dartmouth College and an MBA from The Wharton School of the University of Pennsylvania. He and his wife, Katie, live outside Philadelphia. They have a daughter, three sons, and a very energetic bunch of grandchildren.

Ram Charan is an adviser, author, professor, and speaker who has spent the past forty years working with the CEOs, boards, and senior executives of top companies around the world. He is renowned for cutting through the complexities of running a business in today's fast-changing environment and providing real-world, highly action-able solutions—the kind of advice you can use Monday morning. Jack Welch, former chairman of GE, said of him, "He has the rare ability to distill the meaningful from the meaningless and transfer it to others in a quiet, effective way."

Charan has coached more than a dozen leaders who went on to become CEOs, and he reaches many more through in-house executive education programs. He has won several teaching awards, including the Bell Ringer award from GE's Crotonville Institute and a best teacher award from Northwestern University. He was among BusinessWeek's top ten resources for in-house executive development programs.

Charan has authored or coauthored more than thirty books that have sold over four million copies and been translated into more than a dozen languages. Four of his books were *Wall Street Journal* best-sellers. *Execution*, written with former Honeywell CEO Larry Bossidy, spent more than 150 weeks on the *New York Times* best-seller list. He also has written for *Harvard Business Review, Fortune, Chief Executive,* and other publications. Among his five previous books on corporate governance are *Boards That Deliver, Boards at Work,* and *Owning Up: The 14 Questions Every Board Member Needs to Ask.* Charan and Dennis Carey are coauthors of *Boards That Lead* (with Michael Useem) and *Talent Wins* (with Dominic Barton).

In 2005 Charan was elected a Distinguished Fellow of the National Academy of Human Resources. In 2010 he was named by *NACD Directorship,* the official magazine of the National Association of Corporate Directors, as one of the Directorship 100, the most influential people in corporate governance and the boardroom. He was a member of the NACD Blue Ribbon Commission on the Governance Committee, and serves or has served on a dozen boards in the United States, Brazil, China, India, Canada, and Dubai.

Dennis Carey is vice chairman of Korn Ferry. He has led CEO succession and board engagement programs for some of the highest-profile companies in the United States, including Ford, Tyco, 3M, Humana,

AT&T, and GSK. He has also led board refreshment initiatives for numerous *Fortune* 500 companies, including complete board formations for corporate spinouts and IPOs. Notable examples are Goldman Sachs, Phillips 66, Covidien, Delphi, TE Connectivity, ADT, and the spinoffs of Otis Elevator and Carrier from the United Technologies Corporation (UTC).

In mergers and acquisitions, Carey has earned a reputation for successfully integrating new talent and reducing the cultural risks attendant to these complex transactions. He measures success by how well his placements perform over time and their impact on long-term shareholder return. He currently serves on the board of directors at Nexii, a green construction technology firm based in Vancouver, British Columbia.

In 1999 Carey founded the CEO Academy as an intensive, two-day refresher course for long-serving CEOs, newer CEOs, and potential successors. Affiliated since 2017 with The Wharton School, the CEO Academy has emerged as the best program of its kind in the United States. Carey founded The Prium in 2008 with the goal of creating an exclusive private forum for the CEOs of America's best-managed companies. Both these organizations have attracted some of the most prominent and thoughtful executives in the country.

Carey has taught governance courses at The Wharton School since 2015 and has held post-doctoral fellowships at Princeton Theological Seminary and the Institute of Politics at Harvard Kennedy School. He has cowritten seven books on board performance, CEO succession, business strategy, and talent and has published more than fifty articles, coauthored by top experts in their fields. Among the coauthors of his three most recent books are the former CEO of McKinsey, the former CEO of Vanguard, and the current director of the Leadership Center at Wharton.